DROPBOX API PROJECT: IMAGES TO SLIDESHOW AUTOMATION

Algorithms, Flowcharts, Code, Code explanation

Inderjeet Singh

CONTENTS

FOLDER AND FILE STRUCTURE

files (folder) -> all-files-listed.txt

                 -> t-shirts-pictures (folder)

                 -> intro-pictures (folder)

                 -> slideshow x (folder)

oauth (folder) -> index.php

                 -> oauth-step2.php

                 -> oauth-step3.php

.htaccess

fireworks2.gif

footer.php

header.php

index.php

jquery-3.7.1.min.js

list-and-download.php

login.php

logout.php

move_files_uploaded.php

process-and-upload.php

OVERALL STEPS INVOLVED

1) First App is created in Dropbox which provides 'client_id', 'client_secret', etc. OAuth2 method is used to authorize app using coding steps mentioned below, under topic 'Oauth2 Setup' and to regenerate access token and refresh token. Refresh tokens do not expire easily and Access Token expire after few hours. So, we can use this refresh token (generated during first time authorization, which needed logins to Dropbox) and can use to create access token again and again using API, whenever we want to run software.

2) In case of normal functioning of software, first of all there is need to login software using email and password provided.

3) After logins, index.php file runs, it have two options either show html form, or start software processing. So, first it shows html form which asks for how many files to process in a batch (for downloading). Its default value is set to 30. In case, files are heavy in Megabytes (MBs), then this value can be set to lower values because higher sized files take longer time to process and this can result in 503 error. So, if 503 error shows, this batch size can be lowered to download and enlist lesser files in one step and then repeat this process until all files downloaded from Dropbox 'intro-pictures' and 't-shirts-pictures' folders to hosting server folders 'intro-pictures' folder and 't-shirts-pictures' folder which are present inside 'files' folder, as mentioned in 'Folder and File Structure' above. Once form's 'Start' button pressed, it take the variable value selected and process second part of the page and we feed various static variables to code like client_id (received during app configuring in Dropbox), client_secret (received during app configuring in Dropbox), team_user_id (once generated by another independent API to gets its value), refresh token (already generated once when App authorized) and 'num' variable value received from form which is a dynamic variable.

4) An API generates 'Access Token' from 'Refresh Token' dynamically, with the help of available variables. And we sends Access Token (newly generated) and 'num' variable received from 'index.php' page, as 'downloading_number' to file 'list-and-download.php'.

5) In next step, 'list-and-download.php' file receives various static variables (whose value are fixed), such as client_id, client_secret, namespace_id (once generated by another independent API), team_user_id and various dynamic variables received from 'index.php' file, which are 'access_token' and 'downloading_number'. These variables are used up in running next API which list all files of 'intro-pictures' folder from Dropbox in the form of 'array'. Then a certain code is written which saves file names in file named 'all-files-listed.txt' one by one and in batches on the basis of 'downloading_number' received from 'index.php' file. For example, if 'downloading_number' value is 30, then it will first check if files currently not listed in 'all-files-listed.txt' file and then maximum of 15 files will be downloaded from 'intro-pictures' folder and maximum of 15 files will be downloaded from 't-shirts-pictures' folder through two separate APIs and their names are also added in in 'all-files-listed.txt' file. This page will refresh automatically after 5 seconds and download and enlist up to 30 files in batch which are pending (not listed in 'all-files-listed.txt' file yet) at once. This will continue to refresh, until files are fully moved to hosting server and listed in 'all-files-listed.txt' file. Once, the certain code verifies that all files of two folders are listed and downloaded, then variable 'access_token' is sent to next file named 'process-and-upload.php'.

6) In file 'process-and-upload.php' file, first various static variables fed in it, like 'client_id', 'client_secret', 'namespace_id', 'team_user_id' and then dynamic variable 'access-token' received in this file, to do further processing. Path of the various folders (like 'intro-pictures', t-shirts-pictures', 'slideshow x') and files (like 'all-files-listed.txt') are received through code and saved in certain variables. First total files in 'intro-pictures' folder is checked if it is greater than 1 and if total files in 't-shirts-pictures' folder is greater than 12. If this condition is met then Software checks further if there are grouped file names in 'intro-pictures' folder, with same numbers, so that they can be put on one slideshow. If there are grouped files, a certain set of code runs otherwise other set of code runs at different places on basis of grouped files condition found ones. Then from folder 'intro-pictures', one or more grouped image file/files selected and from 't-shirts-pictures' folder 12 random files are selected and moved to 'slideshow x' folder in server. After that a certain code converts this folder to zip format. This zip file is uploaded to Dropbox's 'slideshow x' folder where it is unzipped automatically through Dropbox's automated function set on 'slideshow x' folder. After that, software waits 7 seconds to complete above process and deletes one file from 'intro-pictures' folder on server whose slideshow has been created, delete all files from 'slideshow x' folder on server, delete zip file on server, then wait for six seconds, so that Dropbox successfully unzipped folder in 'slideshow x' folder in Dropbox. After that another API moves the files to folder in 'Slideshow created' on Dropbox and deletes zip file and folder from 'slideshow x' folder on Dropbox. Then software checks if there are pending files in 'intro-pictures' folder on server, then repeat all steps of step 5 to create next slideshow. One image from 'intro-pictures' folder get deleted every time whenever a slideshow is created, when there are no more files inside 'intro-pictures' folder, then software sends 'access_token' to next file named 'move_files_uploaded.php'.

7) In 'move_files_uploaded.php' file, various required static variables and dynamic variable 'access_token' is passed. At this step, software checks if there are any pending Slideshows which failed to move from 'slideshow x' folder on Dropbox to 'Slideshows created' folder, because some heavy files delay unzipping process in 'Slideshow x' folder on Dropbox and software fail to find the folder to be moved to 'Slideshows created' folder in earlier stages of software working. Software checks for any pending processing in final step and completes it and displays the message of 'Finished creating slideshows.' along with any other pending steps performed.

NUMBERING AND FLOWCHART SYMBOLS

Algorithms and flowchart are shown at bottom of each file's coding. Algorithms are step by step approach in simple English language to elaborate flow of coding.

Steps marked in algorithms are not same as numbers marked in sub-topic 'Code' because numbers marked in 'Code' depicts a particular set of code doing one operation, which is explained below in separate steps in topic 'Code explanation', while it may have multiple sub-steps which are numbered differently in algorithms. So, the numbers marked under sub-topic 'Code' are linked to next sub-topic 'Code explanation' only.

Flowcharts are using diagrams, structures and flow lines to represent flow of code in different conditions. There are various symbols used in Flowcharts as mentioned below. It includes,

1) Oval Box:

This oval box is used at beginning and end of flowchart. It has only two values 'START' and 'END'.

2) Rectangular Box:

This rectangular box has been used to represent ongoing processing of program. It is repeated multiple times. Its structure is shown below,

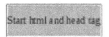

3) Parallelogram Box:

This parallelogram type of box is used to depict input and output of information. Either we add some new data to program or some data goes out of program, it is shown in this type of box. Parallelogram box used is shown below,

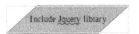

4) Diamond Shaped Box:

This type of box is used to show conditional statements. It could include conditional statements like if, else, for loop, etc. Diamond shaped box is also known as 'decision box'. Its digram used is shown below,

5) Flow Lines:

Flow lines are arrows used to display flow of data and information in a certain direction. It usually move downwards towards next processes. Flow lines structure is shown below,

6) Connectors:

A connector is a small circle which contains a letter. It is mainly used to display where the flow of program goes, if flowchart is bigger than one page. In next page where flow of code is starting, it will have same connector letter in a small circle, as shown below,

DROPBOX APP DETAILS

D ropbox app works on the basis of first a Dropbox app needs created at https://www.dropbox.com/developers/ apps after login to Dropbox account.

We have created an app named 'db2db' which is functional for software. This app has provided following variables:

Client id: demo_client_id

Client Secret: demo_client_secret

Access Token: (Temporary, expires in few hours)

Permissions scopes: Permissions scopes of Dropbox App has been set for Team access.

Redirect URI: https://**your-domain.com**/projects/dropbox-to-dropbox/oauth/oauth-step2.php

Info: If want to generate new access token, it can be generated from one of the following steps:

1) Through app page https://www.dropbox.com/developers/ apps.

2) Through Dropbox API if 'Refresh Token' and other variables available.

3) Through https://your-domain.com/projects/dropbox-to-dropbox/oauth/ , with admin's Dropbox logins. New access token and refresh token get saved in app database using code mentioned in next topic 'Oauth2 Setup'.

OAUTH2 SETUP

To authorize app, this code needs to run at least once when app is created. We can receive 'Refresh Token' from it and 'Access Token'. While access token expires after few hours and needs regenerated, 'Refresh Token' do not expire during a long span of time. 'Oauth2' method required the person should login to Dropbox account, to authorize app again and again to receive fresh access token (however after authorizing app ones, we will be using an API, which can use 'Refresh Token' to generate 'Access Token' again and again whenever software runs so that in place of manually authorizing app every time, we can generate new Access Token through code.)

Index.php

First a file is created, named 'index.php' inside folder named 'oauth'. This file should include 'client_id' and 'redirect url' received from Dropbox app's initial setup.

Algorithm

Step 1: Start

Step 2: Declare variables client_id, redirect_url and authorization_url

Step 3: Create structure of authorization_url

Step 4: Send authorization_url to Dropbox

Step 5: Stop

Flowchart

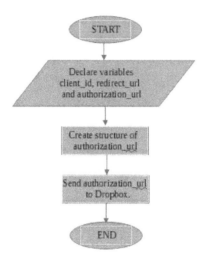

Code

```php
<?php 1)


$client_id = 'demo_client_id'; 2)
$redirect_url = 'https://your-domain.com/projects/dropbox-to-dropbox/oauth/oauth-step2.php';


$authorization_url = 'https://www.dropbox.com/oauth2/authorize?client_id=' .
    $client_id
. '&token_access_type=offline'
. '&response_type=code'
. '&redirect_uri=' . $redirect_url 3)
```

<u>Code Explanation</u>

1) *<?php*

Start PHP tag.

2)   *$client_id = 'demo_client_id';*

   $redirect_url =

      'https://your-domain.com/projects/dropbox-to-dropbox/oauth/oauth-step2.php';

Include value of 'client_id' and 'redirect_url' as received from Dropbox app as mentioned in topic 'Dropbox App Details'

3)   *$authorization_url = 'https://www.dropbox.com/oauth2/authorize?client_id=' .*

   $client_id

   .   *'&token_access_type=offline'*

   .   *'&response_type=code'*

   .   *'&redirect_uri=' . $redirect_url*

Form a URL using variable 'authorization_url'. It includes path to dropbox ' https://www.dropbox.com/oauth2/authorize'. We pass value of 'client_id', token_access_type as offline, response_type as code and redirect_uri.

This will send data from Dropbox to file oauth-step2.php.

Oauth-Step2.Php

Oauth-step2.php will be the file were Dropbox redirect us when we sign in and authorize the App. Note that you would have to enter your database user, password, and name before running this file.

Algorithm

Step 1: Start

Step 2: Declare variable code

Step 3: Initialize code with data received from Dropbox

Step 4: If data received is empty
Declare variables error and error_description to get details
If data received in variable error
Display error and error_description
Stop any further execution of code.

Step 5: Declare variable client_id, secret, redirect_uri, url and data

Step 6: Initialize variable data using code, redirect_uri and grant_type = authorization_code

Step 7: Declare variable query_string and ch for creating API

Step 7: Send variable data to Dropbox API using query_string, url, secret and ch

Step 8: Declare variable response to receive API response.

Step 9: Declare variable json to convert response from JSON to array format

Step 10: If json is null

Display response

Stop any further execution of code.

Step 11: If json has error_summary

Display json error_summary

Stop any further execution of code.

Step 12: If json has error_description

Display error_description

Stop any further execution of code.

Step 13: If json has empty access_token

Display unknown error and response

Stop any further execution of code.

Step 14: Create table dropbox_settings in database

Step 15: Database table has columns: id, access_token, expires_in, token_type, scope,

refresh_token, account_id, uid

Step 16: Set id as primary key of table dropbox_settings which increments automatically and

never null

Step 17: Declare variable host, user, pass, db

Step 18: Declare variable mysqli to connect database using host, user, pass and db

Step 19: Declare variable sql to run insert query on data received from API to database table dropbox_settings

Step 20: Close database connection mysqli.

Flowchart

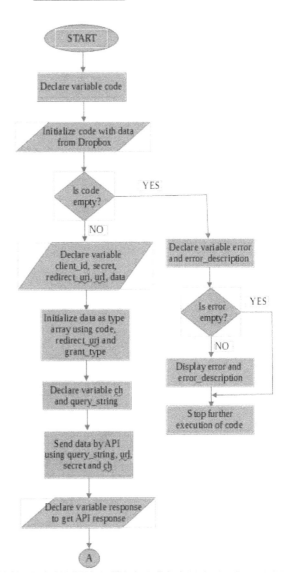

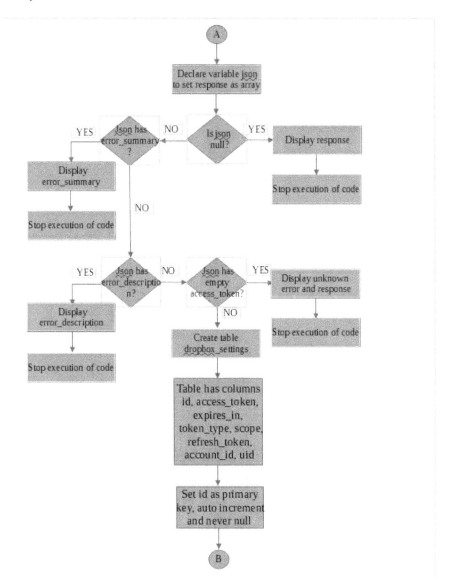

Code

<?php[1]

```php
$code = $_GET['code'];(2)
if (empty($code)) {


   $error = $_GET['error'];(3)
   $error_description = $_GET['error_description'];


   if (!empty($error)) {(4)
      echo $error . ':' . $error_description;
   }


exit;(5)
}


$client_id = 'demo_client_id';(6)
$secret = 'demo_client_secret';
$redirect_url = 'http://localhost/dropbox-api/oauth-step2.php';
$url = 'https://api.dropbox.com/oauth2/token';


$data = array((7)
   'code' => $code,
   'grant_type' => 'authorization_code',
   'redirect_uri' => $redirect_url
```

```php
);

$query_string = http_build_query($data); (8)

$ch = curl_init($url);

curl_setopt($ch, CURLOPT_USERPWD, $client_id . ":" . $secret);

curl_setopt($ch, CURLOPT_POST, true);

curl_setopt($ch, CURLOPT_POSTFIELDS, $query_string);

curl_setopt($ch, CURLOPT_RETURNTRANSFER, true);

$response = curl_exec($ch);

curl_close($ch);


$json = json_decode($response); (9)


if (is_null($json)) { (10)

    echo $response;

    exit;

}


if (!empty($json->error->{".tag"})) { (11)

    echo        $json->error->{".tag"}        .        (!empty($json-
>error_summary) ? ':

    ' . $json->error_summary : ''));

    exit;

}

if (!empty($json->error)) { (12)
```

```php
    echo $json->error . (!empty($json->error_description) ? ':
    ' . $json->error_description :   '');
    exit;
}


if (empty($json->access_token)) {
```
⁽¹³⁾
```php
    echo 'Unknown error:' . $response;
    exit;
}


CREATE TABLE `dropbox_settings` (
```
⁽¹⁴⁾
```sql
    `id` int(11) NOT NULL,
    `access_token` varchar(255) NOT NULL,
    `expires_in` int(11) NOT NULL,
    `token_type` varchar(25) NOT NULL,
    `scope` text NOT NULL,
    `refresh_token` varchar(255) NOT NULL,
    `account_id` varchar(255) NOT NULL,
    `uid` varchar(15) NOT NULL
) ENGINE=InnoDB DEFAULT CHARSET=utf8;


ALTER TABLE `dropbox_settings` ADD PRIMARY KEY (`id`);
```
⁽¹⁵⁾
```sql
ALTER TABLE `dropbox_settings` MODIFY `id` int(11) NOT
NULL AUTO_INCREMENT;
```

```
$host = 'localhost'; (16)
$user = 'YOUR USER';
$pass = 'YOUR PASSWORD';
$db = 'YOUR DATABASE';


$mysqli = new mysqli($host, $user, $pass, $db); (17)


$sql = 'insert into dropbox_settings (access_token, expires_in, token_type, scope,
refresh_token, account_id, uid)
values (
    "' . $mysqli->real_escape_string($json->access_token) . '",
    "' . intval($json->expires_in) . '",
    "' . $mysqli->real_escape_string($json->token_type) . '",
    "' . $mysqli->real_escape_string($json->scope) . '",
    "' . $mysqli->real_escape_string($json->refresh_token) . '",
    "' . $mysqli->real_escape_string($json->account_id) . '",
    "' . intval($json->uid) . '"
)'; (18)


$mysqli->query($sql) or die($mysqli->error); (19)
$mysqli->close();
```

header('Location: oauth-step3.php'); [20)]

Code Explanation

1) *<?php*

   Start PHP tag.

2) *$code = $_GET['code'];*

   if (empty($code)) {

Receive value of variable code using '$_GET' method. After that verify using 'empty()' function that if value of variable 'code' is empty, then move to step 3) and if it is not empty, then step 6) will run.

3)   *$error = $_GET['error'];*

      $error_description = $_GET['error_description'];

This code gets value stored in 'error' using '$_GET' function in '$error' variable. And after that '$_GET' is used to get value of 'error_description' and stored in variable '$error_description'.

4)   *if (!empty($error)) {*

         echo $error . ':' . $error_description;

      }

Next part of code verifies using 'if()' condition and '!empty()' function that if value of variable '$error' is not empty. If it is found not empty, then display value of '$error' and '$error_description' as received in step 3).

5)   *exit;*

After that 'exit' has been added, so that next part of code will not execute, in case variable 'code' is found empty in step 2).

6)   *$client_id = 'demo_client_id';*

      $secret = 'demo_client_secret';

      $redirect_url   =   'http://localhost/dropbox-api/oauth-step2.php';

      $url = 'https://api.dropbox.com/oauth2/token';

This code has been used to add variable values '$client_id', '$secret' and '$redirect_url' as set in Dropbox app, as mentioned under topic 'Dropbox App Details'. And another variable '$url' has been added, which will be used later in code to run API, in step 8).

7)   *$data = array(*

         'code' => $code,

> *'grant_type' => 'authorization_code',*
>
> *'redirect_uri' => $redirect_url*
>
> *);*

In this part of code, an array() has been created using 'code' as variable '$code' as received in step 2), 'redirect_uri' as variable '$redirect_url' as set in step 6) and 'grant_type' is set as 'authorization_code'.

8) *$query_string = http_build_query($data);*

> *$ch = curl_init($url);*
>
> *curl_setopt($ch, CURLOPT_USERPWD, $client_id . ":" . $secret);*
>
> *curl_setopt($ch, CURLOPT_POST, true);*
>
> *curl_setopt($ch, CURLOPT_POSTFIELDS, $query_string);*
>
> *curl_setopt($ch, CURLOPT_RETURNTRANSFER, true);*
>
> *$response = curl_exec($ch);*
>
> *curl_close($ch);*

In this step, a variable '$query_string' has been declared using function 'http_build_query()' which converts value of variable '$data' of type array to the form of a URL-encoded query string and saves it in variable '$query_string'.

After that variable '$ch' has been declared which is includes a function 'curl_init()' with value of variable '$url' in it as set in step 6). This function has been used to initiates a new session at path, which is mentioned in variable '$url'.

After that 'curl_setopt()' function has been used to set various conditions using '$ch' variable, as follows,

CURLOPT_USERPWD has been set to '$client_id' and '$secret'.

CURLOPT_POST has been set to true, to send data using 'POST' method.

CURLOPT_POSTFIELDS has been used to data, which was in variable '$query_string'.

CURLOPT_RETURNTRANSFER has been set to true, to get output from API.

In the end response has been generated by API using function 'curl_exec()' with the help of variable '$ch' and it has been stored in variable '$response'.

After that API session has been closed using 'curl_close()' function, with the help of '$ch' variable.

9) *$json = json_decode($response);*

In this code value of variable '$response' has been converted from JSON to array format using 'json_decode()' function and it is stored in variable '$json'.

10) *if (is_null($json)) {*

 echo $response;

 exit;

}

In this code, it has been verified using 'if()' condition that if value of variable '$json' is null using 'is_null()' function. If it is null, then it display value of variable '$response' which was generated in step 8).

After that 'exit' has been used, which avoids processing of any further code of file.

11) *if (!empty($json->error->{".tag"})) {*

 echo $json->error->{".tag"} . (!empty($json->error_summary) ? ':

  '. $json->error_summary : ");

 exit;

}

In this code, it has been checked using 'if()' condition and '!

empty()' function that value of '.tag' at path 'error' in variable '$json is not empty.

If the value of '.tag' is not empty, then it displays output stored at '.tag'. After that it checks that value of 'error_summary' in variable '$json' using '!empty()' function that, if it is not empty, then display value of 'error_summary'.

After that 'exit' has been used to stop execution of any further code.

12) *if (!empty($json->error)) {*

  echo $json->error . (!empty($json->error_description) ? ':

   ' . $json->error_description : '');

  exit;

 }

In this code, it has been verified using 'if()' condition that if value of 'error' in variable '$json' is not empty.

In the next part of code, it displays value stored at 'error' in '$json' variable. After that code verifies using '!empty()' function that value of 'error_description' in variable '$json' is not empty, then display value of 'error_description.

In next part of code 'exit' has been used to stop execution any further code.

13) *if (empty($json->access_token)) {*

  echo 'Unknown error:' . $response;

  exit;

 }

In this code, 'if()' condition has been used with 'empty()' function to check if value of 'access_token' is empty in variable '$json', then display message 'Unknown error' along with output of variable '$response' which was generated in step 8).

After that 'exit' has been used, to stop any further execution of code.

14) *CREATE TABLE `dropbox_settings` (*

    `id` int(11) NOT NULL,

    `access_token` varchar(255) NOT NULL,

    `expires_in` int(11) NOT NULL,

    `token_type` varchar(25) NOT NULL,

    `scope` text NOT NULL,

    `refresh_token` varchar(255) NOT NULL,

    `account_id` varchar(255) NOT NULL,

    `uid` varchar(15) NOT NULL

) ENGINE=InnoDB DEFAULT CHARSET=utf8;

This is an SQL type of code. This query code has been mentioned here which need to be run directly inside phpmyadmin database's 'sql' section. If this code is run there, it will create a table named 'dropbox_settings' in that database.

Various columns will be added to database table, which includes 'id' whose values can not be null, it can only be of type integer and have maximum length of up to eleven digits.

Another column named 'access_token' it can have maximum length of 255 characters. Its value can not be null. It can hold any time character value which could be numbers, letters, etc.

Another column named 'access_token' has been added. It can have maximum length of eleven digits. It can only be of type integer. It's value can not be null.

Another column named 'expires_in' has been added. It can have value of only integer type. It can have maximum of eleven digits and it's value can not be null.

Another column named 'token_type' has been added. Its value can be of any character type such as number, letter, etc. It's maximum length is set to 25. It's value can not be null.

Another column named 'scope' has been added. It can have value of type 'text'. It's value can not be null.

Another column named 'refresh_token' has been added. It's value can be of any time, such as numbers, letters, etc. It's maximum character length is set to 255. It's value can not be null.

Another column named 'account_id' has been added. It's value can be of any type, such as numbers, letters, etc. It can have maximum character length of 255. It's value can not be null.

Another column named 'uid' has been added. It's value can be of any type, such as numbers, letters, etc. It can have a maximum character length of 25. It's value can not be null.

After that storage engine 'InnoDB' has been used. After that 'charset' or character set encoding has been set to 'utf8'. UTF refers to Unicode Transformation Format. UTF represents characters in unit of one byte. Value of one byte is 8 bits. So, it is named as UTF-8.

15) *ALTER TABLE `dropbox_settings` ADD PRIMARY KEY (`id`);*

ALTER TABLE `dropbox_settings` MODIFY `id` int(11) NOT NULL

AUTO_INCREMENT;

This part of code can only run in phpmyadmin database's 'sql' section. This code has been used to alter changes in table created in step 14).

First, column name 'id' has been set as primary key. A primary key has certain properties such as it can have only unique values. It can not have duplicate values.

Next 'ALTER' query has been used to modify column 'id' to integer type. It can have maximum of 11 integers. It's value can not be null. It is set to auto increment. Auto increments refers to that when a new row entered in table 'dropbox_settings', value of id will be automatically increased by 1 and saved in row.

16) *$host = 'localhost';*

$user = 'YOUR USER';

$pass = 'YOUR PASSWORD';

$db = 'YOUR DATABASE';

In this code, we have set four variables. It includes '$host' whose value is usually 'localhost'. In case of variable '$user' it is value of username. In case of '$pass', it is value of password. In case of '$db', it is name of database.

17) *$mysqli = new mysqli($host, $user, $pass, $db);*

In this code, value of variable '$mysqli' has been set. It includes function 'mysqli()' which uses value of variables '$host', '$user', '$pass' and '$db' as set in step 16).

18) *$sql = 'insert into dropbox_settings (access_token, expires_in, token_type,*

> *scope, refresh_token, account_id, uid) values (*
>
> *'" . $mysqli->real_escape_string($json->access_token) . "',*
>
> *'" . intval($json->expires_in) . "',*
>
> *'" . $mysqli->real_escape_string($json->token_type) . "',*
>
> *'" . $mysqli->real_escape_string($json->scope) . "',*
>
> *'" . $mysqli->real_escape_string($json->refresh_token) . "',*
>
> *'" . $mysqli->real_escape_string($json->account_id) . "',*
>
> *'" . intval($json->uid) . "'*

)';

In this code, a variable '$sql' has been declared. Inside this variable a mysqli query has been run, which is used to insert value of 'access_token', 'expires_in', 'token_type', 'scope', 'refresh_token' and 'uid' on the basis of various values received from variable '$json'.

In this query, various functions has been used such as 'real_escape_string()' and 'intval()'. Function 'real_escape_string()' has been used in case of '$json->access_token', '$json->token_type', '$json->scope', '$json->refresh_token', '$json->account_id', which is used to remove any special characters inside variable's value. Second function 'intval()' has been used, which is used to get only integer value, in case of variable values '$json->expires_in' and '$json->uid'.

19) *$mysqli->query($sql) or die($mysqli->error);*

    $mysqli->close();

In this code, variable '$mysqli' has been used which was created in step 17) to create database connection and 'query()' function has been used to run the mysqli query mentioned in variable '$sql' in step 18). 'or' has been been used to link alternative output. Another function 'die()' has been used, in case there is an error at 'error' in variable '$mysqli'. 'die()' function shows the error message and stop any further execution of code.

In next part of code, 'close()' function has been to close the connection created in variable '$mysqli' in step 17).

20) *header('Location: oauth-step3.php');*

In this code, function 'header()' has been used. 'header()' function has been used to redirect the page to next file 'oauth-step3.php'.

Oauth-Step3.Php

The last file on our process displays an Authorization Successful message. This is a simple HTML code file.

Algorithm

Step 1: Start

Step 2: Start html tag

Step 3: Start and stop head tag

Step 4: Start body tag

Step 5: Start div tag

Step 6: Start and stop paragraph tag p with text: My Dropbox App

Step 7: Start and stop strong tag with text: Authorization Successful

Step 8: Stop div tag

Step 9: Stop body tag

Step 10: Stop html tag

Step 11: Stop

Flowchart

<u>Code</u>

```
<html>1)

    <head></head>2)

    <body>3)

        <div style="text-align:center">4)

            <p>My Dropbox App</p>5)

            <strong>Authorization Successful</strong>6)

        </div>7)
    </body>
</html>
```

Code Explanation

1) *\<html\>*

First start 'html' tag. It is added only as per HTML file structure of tags.

2) *\<head\>\</head\>*

Start and stop 'head' tag. This is a simple file, so only HTML file structure followed and no need to add anything in these tags.

3) *\<body\>*

After that start 'body' tag, as per need of HTML file structure.

4) *\<div style="text-align:center"\>*

Inside 'body' tag, which was started in step 3), 'div' tag has been created. Inside 'div' tag inline CSS style has been added. Here CSS is set to align text in 'div' tag, in centre of page.

5) *\<p\>My Dropbox App\</p\>*

Inside 'div' tag, which was created in step 4), 'p' tag has been added. Here 'p' tag refers to paragraph tag. This tag is used to display formatting of text inside this code to look like paragraph. For example, text added outside 'p' tag will be automatically moved to next line, etc. Inside 'p' tag, text has been added 'My Dropbox App'. Its output is shown below,

My Dropbox App

Here we can see that text is centre aligned because of inline style set in step 4).

6) *\<strong\>Authorization Successful\</strong\>*

In this code, 'strong' tag has been started. 'strong' tag makes the text to look bold. In 'strong' tag 'Authorization Successful' has been added, it will show as below,

Authorization Successful

In above output, we can see that 'Authorization Successful' has been added in centre of page. It is under the affect of inline CSS, added in step 4).

7)   *</div>*

</body>

</html>

In this code, we can see that 'div' tag, which was started in step 4), has been closed. In the next part of code 'body' tag which was started in step 3), has been closed. In the next part of code, 'html' tag which was started in step 1), has been closed.

SOFTWARE OPERATIONS

S oftware is created in PHP programming language. Other languages used in combination are HTML, CSS and Jquery, PHP, Regex. Software runs at URL: https://your-domain.com/projects/dropbox-to-dropbox

HEADER.PHP

'header.php' file contains common code which is included on top of other files. It includes navigation menu bar, designing shared in all pages in style <style> </style> tags. Script shared in all pages, HTML head '<head> </head>', '<body>', etc. Tags. We can include this file in other files using 'include()' function of PHP. Various steps performed to create coding of header.php file has been explained using algorithm below

Algorithm

Step 1: Start

Step 2: Start HTML and head tag

Step 3: Catch and display any errors present

Step 4: Include Jquery library

Step 5: Start script tag

Step 6: Declare variable url as current URL

Step 7: If any link of anchor tag match url,
        Add 'active' class to relevant li tag

Step 8: Stop script tag and start style tag

Step 9: Add CSS code for .button, ul, li, li a, li a:hover, .active

Step 10: Stop style tag and start body tag and ul tag

Step 11: Add li tags and anchor tags with URL links

Step 12: Stop ul tag

Step 13: Stop

Flowchart

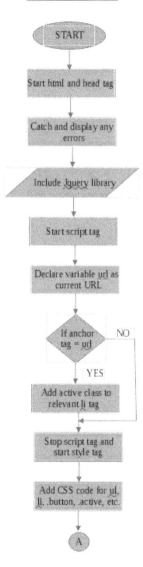

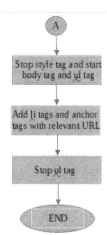

Code

```
<!DOCTYPE html> 1)
  <head>

    <?php                ini_set('display_errors',        1);
ini_set('display_startup_errors', 1);
      error_reporting(E_ALL); ?> 2)


    <script src="jquery-3.7.1.min.js"></script> 3)

    <script type="text/javascript"> 4)
    $(document).ready(function () {
      var url = window.location;
      $('ul.nav a[href="'+ url +'"]').parent().addClass('active');
      $('ul.nav a').filter(function() {
        return this.href == url;
      }).parent().addClass('active');
    });
  </script>
    <style> 5)
    .button{
      background:aliceblue;
      padding-top: 12px;
      padding-bottom: 12px;
      padding-left: 32px;
      padding-right: 32px;
    }
    ul {

        list-style-type: none;
      margin: 0;
      padding: 0;
```

```
    overflow: hidden;
    background-color: #333;
   }
   li {
    float: left;
   }
   li a {
     display: block;

        color: white;
     text-align: center;
     padding: 14px 16px;
     text-decoration: none;
   }
   li a:hover {
    background-color: #111;
   }
   .active {4)
     background-color:#111;
   }
  </style>

 </head>6)
 <body>

  <ul class="nav navbar-nav">7)
    <li><a href="https://your-domain.com/projects/dropbox-to-
dropbox/index.php">Home</a>
      </li>
    <li><a
       href="https://your-domain.com/projects/dropbox-to-
dropbox/move_files_uploaded.php"
       target="_blank">Move files Uploaded</a></li>
    <li style="float:right;"><a
       href="https://your-domain.com/projects/dropbox-to-
dropbox/logout.php">Logout</a></li>
```

```
</ul>
```

Code Explanation

1) *<!DOCTYPE html>*
   <head>

First HTML tag is started and head tag <head> tag is applied.

2)   *<?php   ini_set('display_errors',   1);*
ini_set('display_startup_errors', 1);
   error_reporting(E_ALL); ?>

This PHP code is used to display detailed warnings and errors in code. If we remove this code, software will not show most of warning or error message.

3) *<script src="jquery-3.7.1.min.js"></script>*

This code is used to run code mentioned in another file named 'jquery-3.7.2.min.js'. Code contained in this file is a ready-made library code, which is used to run 'Jquery' type of code in files.

4) *<script type="text/javascript">*
     $(document).ready(function () {
       var url = window.location;
       $('ul.nav a[href="'+ url +'"]').parent().addClass('active');
       $('ul.nav a').filter(function() {
         return this.href == url;
       }).parent().addClass('active');
     });
   </script>

This is Jquery code enclosed in script <script type="text/javascript"> </script> tags. Jquery works on coding methods of Javascript. It is used to add class 'active' inside current menu bar's code. So that active menu bar's background colour get changed.

To apply changed background colour to any element which have class 'active', is mentioned in CSS code mentioned in style <style></style> tags, using Hex colour code #111.

Below is how this Hex code has been applied using CSS,

```
.active {
    background-color:#111;
}
```

5) <style>
```
.button{
background:aliceblue;
padding-top: 12px;
padding-bottom: 12px;
padding-left: 32px;
padding-right: 32px;
}

  ul {
list-style-type: none;
margin: 0;
      padding: 0;
  overflow: hidden;
  background-color: #333;
}
li {
 float: left;
}
li a {
  display: block;
  color: white;
  text-align: center;
  padding: 14px 16px;
  text-decoration: none;
}
```

```
  li a:hover {
   background-color: #111;
  }
  .active {
    background-color:#111;
  }
 </style>
```

Code mentioned in <style> </style> tags is CSS (Cascading Style Sheets) code and is used to do designing of various elements of software, such as buttons, navigation bar, etc. using certain CSS properties applied to different elements.

Designing on all buttons of website has been done as follows,

```
 .button{
 background:aliceblue;
 padding-top: 12px;
 padding-bottom: 12px;
 padding-left: 32px;
 padding-right: 32px;
 }
```

Here 'background color' of button has been set to 'aliceblue'. There is padding added around the button, as shown in this code.

CSS code shown below, is linked to navigation bar,

```
 ul {
 list-style-type: none;
 margin: 0;
     padding: 0;
 overflow: hidden;
 background-color: #333;
```

```
      }
      li {
        float: left;
      }
      li a {
        display: block;
        color: white;
        text-align: center;
        padding: 14px 16px;
        text-decoration: none;
      }
      li a:hover {
        background-color: #111;
      }
```

This CSS code is linked to various HTML tags, set in step 7).

6) *</head>*
   <body>

After that head tag has been closed </head> and body tag <body> has been started.

7) *<ul class="nav navbar-nav">*
   <li><a href="https://your-domain.com/projects/dropbox-to-dropbox/index.php">Home</a>
   </li>
   <li><a
   href="https://your-domain.com/projects/dropbox-to-dropbox/move_files_uploaded.php"
   target="_blank">Move files Uploaded</a></li>
   <li style="float:right;"><a
   href="https://your-domain.com/projects/dropbox-to-dropbox/logout.php">Logout</a></li>
   </ul>

After that, this code has been used to create navigation bar (or menu bar). Various HTML tags has been used to create this navigation bar. Following is the list of HTML tags used to create navigation bar,

<ul> </ul> // It represents 'unordered list'

<li> </li> // It represents 'list item'

<a href= ""> </a> // It represents 'Anchor' tag, which contain links to pages where

*   // button click will open pages*

target = "_blank" // It refers to page will open in new tab in browser

style= "float:right;" // It is inline type of CSS code to display element, at right side of

*   // page*

Here '<ul>' tags are at outer side, which holds 3 '<li>' tags and each '<li>' tag holds an 'Anchor' tag. Designing of these elements has been done in step 5) using internal CSS in '<style>' tags.

FOOTER.PHP

'footer.php' file will be called at bottom of code of many other pages of software where 'header.php' file was included. This file is required because it closes main HTML tags of page which were started in 'header.php' file. 'footer.php' file includes code which refers to common footer section of pages. Footer section can be used to add anything in end of the pages at ones.

Algorithm

Step 1: Start

Step 2: Stop body tag

Step 3: Stop html tag

Step 4: Stop

Flowchart

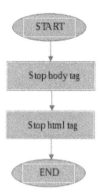

Code

```
</body> 1)
</html> 2)
```

Code Explanation

1)   *</body>*

In this code, 'body' tag has been closed. 'body' tag was opened in 'header.php' file.

2) *</html>*

In this code, main 'html' tag which started at top of 'header.php' file has been closed.

LOGIN.PHP

'login.php file is used to create login methods of software. Login uses 'cookies' method to verify in each page if user is logged in or not.

Algorithm

Step 1: Start

Step 2: Include header file

Step 3: Read cookie value

Step 4: If cookie value is set
    Declare baseURL as homepage URL
    Redirect to baseURL
     Else
    Display empty character

Step 5: Declare HTML form
        Declare Input type username, password and submit button

Step 6: Enter username, password and click submit button

Step 7: If username & password are set and not empty
    Declare username and password
     Else
    Display 'Please enter logins'

Step 8: If username and password match for first user
    Declare cookie variable as user for 43200 seconds

Declare baseURL as homepage URL
Redirect to baseURL

Elseif username and password values match for second user

Declare cookie variable as user for 43200 seconds
Declare baseURL as homepage URL
Redirect to baseURL

Else
Display 'Logins incorrect'

Step 9: Include footer file

Stop 10: Stop

Flowchart

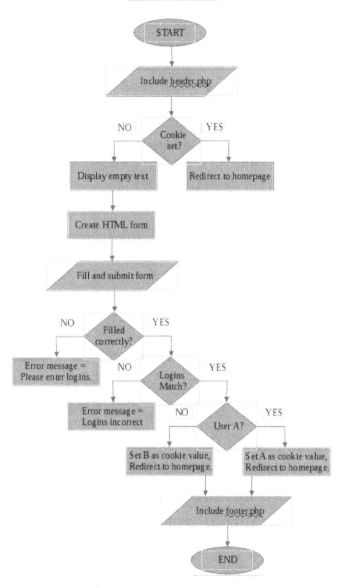

Code

```php
<?php

    include('header.php');

    if(isset($_COOKIE['user'])) {
      $baseURL = 'https://your-domain.com/projects/dropbox-to-dropbox';
      header("Location: $baseURL");
    } else {
      echo ";
    }

    if(isset($_POST['username']) && !empty($_POST['username']) &&
        isset($_POST['password'])              &&            !
empty($_POST['password'])){
      $username = $_POST['username'];
      $password = $_POST['password'];

      if($username == "demo_name1@gmail.com" && $password ==
        "demo_password1"){
      setcookie('user', $username, time() + (43200), "/");
      $baseURL = 'https://your-domain.com/projects/dropbox-to-dropbox';
      header("Location: $baseURL");

      } elseif($username == "demo_name2@gmail.com" &&
$password ==
        "demo_password2"){
      setcookie('user', $username, time() + (43200), "/");
      $baseURL = 'https://your-domain.com/projects/dropbox-to-dropbox';
```

```php
        header("Location: $baseURL");

    } else {⁽⁸⁾
        echo "<br><br><br><div><center>Logins incorrect.</center></div>";
    }
} else {⁽⁹⁾
    echo "<br><br><br><div><center>Please enter logins</center></div>";
}


echo '<center>';⁽⁴⁾
echo '<br><br><br>';
echo '<form action="" method="POST">';
    echo 'Enter Username:';
            echo '<input type="email" name="username" placeholder="Your email"
        required><br>';
    echo 'Enter Password:';
            echo '<input type="password" name="password" placeholder="Password"
        required><br>';
echo '<br>';
echo '<input type="submit" class="button">';
echo '</form>';
echo '</center>';

include('footer.php');⁽¹⁰⁾
?>
```

<u>Code Explanation</u>

1) *<?php*

On top of the code first PHP tags are started, below which PHP programming language code can be written.

2) *include('header.php');*

After that 'header.php' file is included using code.

3) *if(isset($_COOKIE['user'])) {*
     $baseURL = 'https://your-domain.com/projects/dropbox-to-dropbox';
     header("Location: $baseURL");
  } else {
    echo '';
  }

After that this code checks if cookie is set. If cookie is set, then login page will be automatically directed to homepage, so in case cookie is set, login page can not be viewed.

4) *echo '<center>';*
    *echo '

';*
    echo '<form action="" method="POST">';
      echo 'Enter Username:';
              echo '<input type="email" name="username" placeholder="Your email"
          *required>
';*
      echo 'Enter Password:';
        echo '<input type="password" name="password" placeholder="Password"
          *required>
';*
      echo '<br>';
      echo '<input type="submit" class="button">';
    echo '</form>';

echo '</center>';

This code has been used near bottom of page, which is used to create a form, where username and password can be entered and submitted. Various tags used in it are listed below,

<center> // All the elements of code which shows on page will display in centre (or
       // middle) of page
*
 // This tag is used to show next part of code in next line*
<form> // This tag is used to create an HTML form
<input> // This tag is used to add different elements of form such as 'textbox',
       // 'submit button', etc.

In the end, these tags has been closed using </center> and </form>

In the <form> tag, action is set to empty, this means that after 'submit' button is clicked, then data filled in form will be sent to current page, where we can verify that data as done in step 5) and after that process that data.

In the <form> tag, 'method' has been set to 'POST'. It means that data can be fetched by code using '$_POST' method.

In first <input> tag, 'type' has been set to 'email'. It means that textbox can only accept an email address including symbol '@' and '.', example, abc@gmail.com. A normal text or numbers will not be accepted. This field has been set to 'required' so that if it is empty, then 'submit' button will not work. 'name' of input type has been set to 'username', it will be used to get value of this field, in step 5).

Similarly, for second <input> tag, 'type' is set to 'password', so anything entered in this text box will be show in form of dots '...' and actual text will be not visible. 'name' has been set to 'password', so, it will be used to get this text box value in step 5). This field is set to 'required', so if this text box is left empty, then 'submit' button will not work.

Third <input> tag, is used to create a button, when this button is pressed, then data filled in form will be sent to step 5). Here 'class' has been set to 'button', it is used to add CSS code in <style> tags in 'header.php' file, so as to do designing on button of form.

5) *if(isset($_POST['username']) && !empty($_POST['username']) &&*
   isset($_POST['password']) && !empty($_POST['password'])){
   $username = $_POST['username'];
   $password = $_POST['password'];

This part of the code runs if username and password in 'form' are filled in step 4) and 'submit' button is pressed. Code gets values of 'username' and 'password' using '$_POST' method. This code verifies if username and password is set using 'isset()' function and not empty using '!empty()' function. If they are set and not empty, then save 'username' value to variable '$username' and save value of 'password' in '$password' variable.

6)   *if($username == "demo_name1@gmail.com" && $password ==*
     "demo_password1"){
     setcookie('user', $username, time() + (43200), "/");
     $baseURL = 'https://your-domain.com/projects/dropbox-to-dropbox';
     header("Location: $baseURL");

This part of code verifies that if value of variable '$username' is equal to {email} and value of variable '$password' is equal to {password}.

In the next part of code, a cookie has been set using 'setcookie()' function. Here cookie's variable name is 'user' and its value is one saved in variable '$username'. Life span of cookie has been set to '43200' seconds (or 12 hours). It means that after 12 hours, any login session will automatically be logged out. Cookie is set and then URL address of home page has been set in variable '$baseURL'. After that code redirects the page to homepage of software using 'header()' function.

7)   } elseif($username == "demo_name2@gmail.com" && $password ==
      "demo_password2"){
      setcookie('user', $username, time() + (43200), "/");
      $baseURL = 'https://your-domain.com/projects/dropbox-to-dropbox';
      header("Location: $baseURL");

This part of code is similar to step 6) and use 'elseif()' condition. So, that if value of variable '$username' and '$password' is same as one mentioned in code, then logins will also work.

In the next part of code, a cookie has been set using 'setcookie()' function. Here cookie's variable name is 'user' and its value is one saved in variable '$username'. Life span of cookie has been set to '43200' seconds (or 12 hours). It means that after 12 hours, any login session will automatically be logged out. Cookie is set and then URL address of home page has been set in variable '$baseURL'. After that code redirects the page to homepage of software using 'header()' function.

8) } else {
      echo "

 Logins incorrect. ";
    }

'else' condition mentioned in code is linked to step 6) and 7). If both step 6) and step 7) fails to work, as per conditions set on of those codes, then this code will run. It will show a message of 'Logins incorrect.'. Output shows at centre of page, as follows,

Logins incorrect.

9) *} else {*

      *echo "

<div><center>Please enter logins</ center></div>";*

    }

This 'else' condition, is linked to step 5). In step, it is verified on top, if 'username' and 'password' is not empty. If it is found, empty, then this 'else' condition will show message 'Please enter logins'. This message also shows when 'login.php' page is opened and logins are not yet submitted and this condition runs.

Here '<br>' tag has been used four times. Each '<br>' tag refers to display output in next line. '<center>' tag makes the text display in middle of page, from left and right. Output shows at centre of page, as follows,

Please enter logins

10) *include('footer.php');*

    ?>

At the end of the page, code of 'footer.php' file has been included using 'include()' function and PHP tag opened at top of page in 'header.php' file, is closed using '?>'.

LOGOUT.PHP

Logout file is linked with button 'Logout' in navigation bar. Algorithm of logout page is shown below,

<u>Algorithm</u>

Step 1: Start

Step 2: Declare variable setcookie as empty

Step 3: Unset cookie variable

Step 4: Declare baseURL as login page URL

Step 5: Redirect to baseURL

Step 6: Stop

Flowchart

Code

```php
<?php①
    setcookie("user","",1,'/');②
  unset($_COOKIE["user"]);

    $baseURL = 'https://your-domain.com/projects/dropbox-to-dropbox/login.php';③
  header("Location: $baseURL");
```

Code Explanation

1) *<?php*

First, PHP tag has been started.

2) *setcookie("user","",1,'/');
unset($_COOKIE["user"]);*

This part of code is used to set the cookie value to empty and has set its life span to one second. After that it 'unset()' function has been used to unset or delete the cookie and its value, in case any variable value is left in cookie variable.

3) *$baseURL = 'https://your-domain.com/projects/dropbox-to-dropbox/login.php';
header("Location: $baseURL");*

This part of code is used to save the login page URL in variable '$baseURL' and 'header()' function has been used to redirect the user to 'login.php' page automatically. This page runs in a fraction of second and directly 'login.php' page shows up.

MAIN SOFTWARE PROCESSING

Main processing of Software, related to functioning of Dropbox APIs to get images from Dropbox, processing of Dropbox images to create Slideshows and to upload Slideshows to Dropbox is done in following files.

INDEX.PHP

This file is linked to 'Home' in navigation bar. This is where main software processing starts. Algorithm of index.php is shown below,

__Algorithm__

Step 1: Start

Step 2: Include header file

Step 3: Get and read cookie value

Step 4: If cookie variable user value is set
    Display message1*
     Else
    Declare variable baseURL as login page URL
    Redirect to baseURL

Step 5: Declare variables client_id, client_secret and team_user_id

Step 6: Start tag names div and center

Step 7: Declare HTML form with method as POST

Step 8: Declare variable num in select tag

Step 9: Increment value of num from 2 to 50

Step 10: If num = 30
    Display 30 and set option tag as selected
     Else

Display option tag with other number

Step 11: Display message2*

Step 12: Set input type as submit for button

Step 13: Close form, div and center tag

Step 14: If num variable is set
run step 15
else
run step 6 to step 13

Step 15: Declare downloading_number as value of num

Step 16: Round off, downloading_number/2

Step 17: Declare variables host, user, pass and db

Step 18: Declare variable connect using variables in step 17, to connect to database

Step 19: Declare variable sql with query to search latest refresh_token from database

Step 20: Declare variable result to run sql with connect

Step 21: Declare variable row and while data in result, assign it to row

Step 22: Declare variable refresh_token, assign value of refresh token from database

Step 23: Step 17 to 22 are commented and will not run repeatedly, unless required

Step 24: Assign predefined value to refresh_token

Step 25: Declare variable curl

Step 26: Assign value of refresh_token, client_id and client_secret to API

Step 27: Declare variable response, assign output of API to variable response

Step 28: Convert response from JSON format to array format

Step 29: If response at path access_token is not empty
Declare variable access_token and assign value to it
Else
Display message3*
Stop next part of code from running
Step 30: Declare variable baseURL as path to file list-and-download.php

Step 31: Redirect to baseURL with variables access_token and downloading_number

Step 32: include file footer.php

Step 33: Stop

message1*: Welcome {user_email}
message2*: (In case of heavy files in Mbs, it is best to keep this limit lower to avoid 503 error)
message3*: Dropbox Access Token missing. It could be because of temporary network error, refresh token may've expired, etc. Please retry after some time or contact this software administrator.

Flowchart

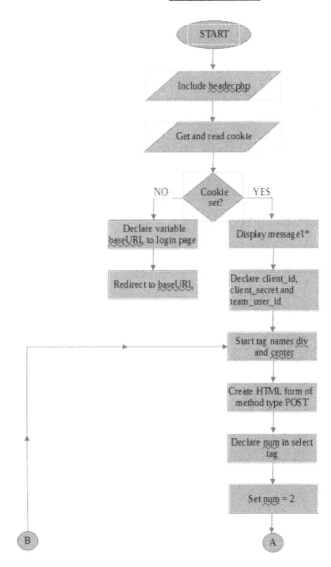

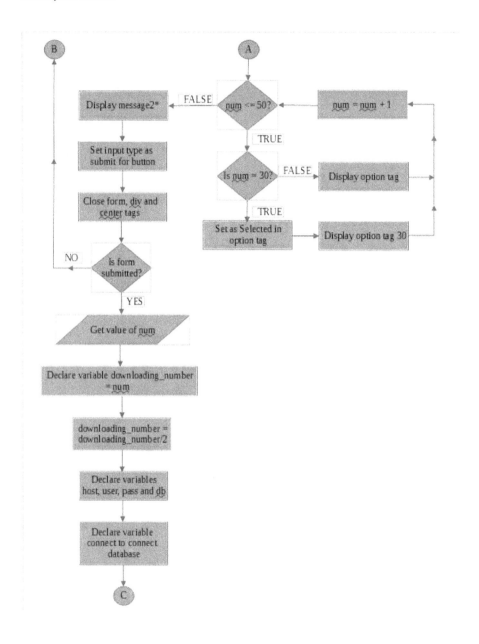

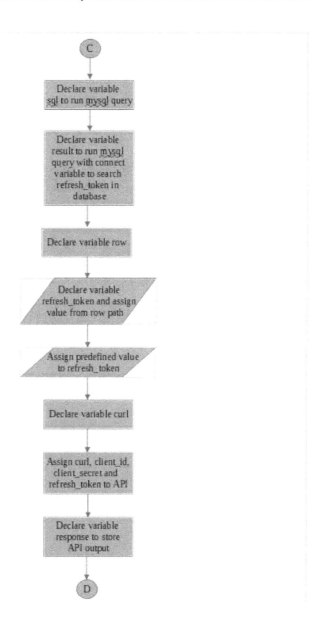

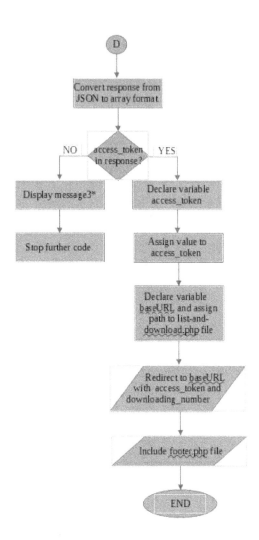

Code

```php
<?php①
include('header.php');

if(isset($_COOKIE['user'])) {②
    echo '<br>  Welcome '.$_COOKIE['user'];
} else {
    $baseURL       =      'https://your-domain.com/projects/
dropbox-to-dropbox/login.php';
    header("Location: $baseURL");
}

$client_id = "demo_client_id";③
$client_secret = "demo_client_secret";
$team_user_id = "demo_team_user_id";

if(isset($_POST['num']) && !empty($_POST['num'])){⑤
    $downloading_number = $_POST['num'];
    $downloading_number                            =
round($downloading_number/2);

    /*⑤
    $host = 'localhost';
    $user = 'database_logins';
    $pass = 'database_logins1A';
    $db = 'database_logins';
    $connect = new mysqli($host, $user, $pass, $db);
    $sql = 'SELECT  refresh_token  FROM  dropbox_settings
ORDER BY id DESC
        LIMIT 1';
    $result = mysqli_query($connect, $sql);
    while($row = mysqli_fetch_assoc($result)){
        $refresh_token = $row['refresh_token'];
    }
    */
```

```php
    $refresh_token =
"demo_refresh_token-
OL";
    $curl = curl_init();
    curl_setopt_array($curl, array(
      CURLOPT_URL   =>  'https://api.dropbox.com/oauth2/
token',
      CURLOPT_RETURNTRANSFER => true,
      CURLOPT_ENCODING => '',
      CURLOPT_MAXREDIRS => 10,
      CURLOPT_TIMEOUT => 0,
      CURLOPT_FOLLOWLOCATION => true,
      CURLOPT_HTTP_VERSION                    =>
CURL_HTTP_VERSION_1_1,
      CURLOPT_CUSTOMREQUEST => 'POST',
      CURLOPT_POSTFIELDS                    =>
'grant_type=refresh_token&refresh_token='.
        $refresh_token.'&client_id='.
$client_id.'&client_secret='.$client_secret.'",
      CURLOPT_HTTPHEADER => array(
        'Content-Type: application/x-www-form-urlencoded'
       ),
    ));
    $response = curl_exec($curl);
    curl_close($curl);
    $response = json_decode($response, true);
    if(!empty($response['access_token'])){
      $access_token = $response['access_token'];
    } else {
      echo "Dropbox Access Token missing. It could be because
of temporary
        network error, refresh token may've expired, etc. Please
retry after some time
        or contact this software administrator.";
      exit;
```

```php
        }

        $baseURL        =        'https://your-domain.com/projects/
dropbox-to-dropbox/list-and-
        download.php'; [8]
        header("Location: $baseURL.'?
        access_token=$access_token&&downloading_number=
$downloading_number");
        exit;

    } else { [4]
        echo '<div>';
            echo '<center>';
                echo '<form action="" method="POST">';
                    echo '<br><br><br>';
                    echo '<label for="cars">Select Downloading
Batch Size:</label>';
                    echo '<select name="num" id="num">';
                        for($num=2; $num<=50; $num++){
                            if($num==30){
                                echo '<option selected="selected"
                                value="'.$num.'">'.$num.'</option>';
                            } else {
                                echo        '<option        value="'.$num.'">'.
$num.'</option>';
                            }
                        }
                    echo '</select>';
                    echo '<div style="font-size:11px;">(In case of
heavy files in MBs, it is
                        best to keep this limit lower to avoid 503
error)</div>';
                    echo '<br>';
                    echo        '<input        type="submit"        value="Start"
class="button">';
                echo '</form>';
```

```
        echo '</center>';
    echo '</div>';
}

include('footer.php');
?>
```

Code Explanation

1) *<?php*
   include('header.php');

First of all PHP tag is started and 'header.php' file is included on top of code.

2) *if(isset($_COOKIE['user'])) {*
   *echo '
 Welcome '.$_COOKIE['user'];*
   } else {
   $baseURL   =   'https://your-domain.com/projects/
   dropbox-to-dropbox/login.php';
   header("Location: $baseURL");
   }

In the next' part of code, it is checked if cookie (which contains login variable) is set, as done in page in 'login.php' file (page 20). If cookie is not set, then 'else' condition run and user is not allowed to view this page, and user will be automatically redirected to the 'login.php' page.

3) *$client_id = "demo_client_id";*
   $client_secret = "demo_client_secret";
   $team_user_id = "demo_team_user_id";

After that we have fed some static variables 'client_id', 'client_secret' and 'team_user_id' in 'index.php' file.

4) *} else {*
   echo '<div>';
   echo '<center>';
   echo '<form action="" method="POST">';
   *echo '

';*
   echo '<label for="cars">Select Downloading
   Batch Size:</label>';
   echo '<select name="num" id="num">';

```
for($num=2; $num<=50; $num++){
    if($num==30){
        echo '<option selected="selected"
            value="'.$num.'">'.$num.'</option>';
    } else {
        echo    '<option    value="'.$num.'">'.
$num.'</option>';
    }
}
echo '</select>';
echo '<div style="font-size:11px;">(In case of
heavy files in MBs, it is
        best to keep this limit lower to avoid 503
error)</div>';
echo '<br>';
echo '<input    type="submit"    value="Start"
class="button">';
echo '</form>';
echo '</center>';
echo '</div>';
}
```

This part of code runs when home page is newly opened. It is part of the 'else' condition. This code is used to create a form with a dropdown which gets value 2 to 50, with a 'Start' button. It has default value set to 30.

5)  ```
if(isset($_POST['num']) && !empty($_POST['num'])){
    $downloading_number = $_POST['num'];
    $downloading_number   =
round($downloading_number/2);
```

If form is submitted by pressing 'Start' button, this condition gets the number value of form and put in the variable '$downloading_number' code to process after dividing it with 2. (It is divided with 2 because later it will be fed in two APIs which get files from 'intro-pictures' folder and 't-shirts-pictures' folder
```

of Dropbox. So, both APIs will process 50% of value in one batch processing.)

6) /*

```
        $host = 'localhost';
        $user = 'database_logins';
        $pass = 'database_logins1A';
        $db = 'database_logins';
        $connect = new mysqli($host, $user, $pass, $db);
        $sql = 'SELECT refresh_token FROM dropbox_settings
ORDER BY id DESC
            LIMIT 1';
        $result = mysqli_query($connect, $sql);
        while($row = mysqli_fetch_assoc($result)){
            $refresh_token = $row['refresh_token'];
        }
    */
```

This code has been put in comments /* and */ and is not used on regular basis. This code can be used if ever the 'Refresh Token' expired by Dropbox, then new Refresh Token can be automatically fetched using this code, if new created by using this link: https://your-domain.com/projects/dropbox-to-dropbox/oauth

```
7) $refresh_token =
    "demo_refresh_token-
      OL";
        $curl = curl_init();
        curl_setopt_array($curl, array(
          CURLOPT_URL => 'https://api.dropbox.com/oauth2/
token',
          CURLOPT_RETURNTRANSFER => true,
          CURLOPT_ENCODING => '',
          CURLOPT_MAXREDIRS => 10,
```

```
        CURLOPT_TIMEOUT => 0,
        CURLOPT_FOLLOWLOCATION => true,
        CURLOPT_HTTP_VERSION                    =>
CURL_HTTP_VERSION_1_1,
        CURLOPT_CUSTOMREQUEST => 'POST',
        CURLOPT_POSTFIELDS                      =>
'grant_type=refresh_token&refresh_token='.
        $refresh_token.'&client_id='.
$client_id.'&client_secret='.$client_secret.",
        CURLOPT_HTTPHEADER => array(
         'Content-Type: application/x-www-form-urlencoded'
        ),
      ));
      $response = curl_exec($curl);
      curl_close($curl);
      $response = json_decode($response, true);
      if(!empty($response['access_token'])){
        $access_token = $response['access_token'];
      } else {
        echo "Dropbox Access Token missing. It could be because
of temporary
            network error, refresh token may've expired, etc.
Please retry after some
            time or contact this software administrator.";
        exit;
      }
```

As mentioned above, 'Access Token' has life span of few hours and it expires automatically after that, so we use this API, to create new 'Access Token' every time software runs from the value of 'Refresh Token' we have already: "demo_refresh_token" and by feeding some other variables in API, like 'client_id' and 'client_secret'.

Response generated in variable '$response' from the above API has been converted from JSON to array form using 'json_decode()' function it looks like as shown below,

[access_token] => demo_access_token
wVd4zWAe4Uaq4sgfAGWkjo9SYnHlg1Y0crzP_AsqSIOCfn8Uyf7a6NX
rLERWfdcxAqUBb
tDCQmVPM5iKGmpRdz9IszmOSLfFJXfWJim0Q0jH_xM4wUz9pBvSO
nf8rNdeyTDSC6Xst-
9mccVX2N-S
[token_type] => bearer
[expires_in] => 14400

After that we put access token at [access_token] inside variable '$access_token', as follows,

$access_token = $response['access_token']

Access Token received in variable '$access_token' can be used later to run rest of the Dropbox APIs in software.

If 'access_token' fail to generate, then 'else' condition works, which shows error message,

Dropbox Access Token missing. It could be because of temporary network error, refresh token may've expired, etc. Please retry after some time or contact this software administrator.

In case the access token failed to generate, then there are three solutions listed for it, under topic 'Dropbox App Details'.

In case 'access_token' generated through Dropbox App, then it has a short life span of only 4 hours until it is valid to use and it needs to be added in code manually.

In case of solution offered to generate 'access_token' through 'refresh_token' and other details, under topic 'Dropbox App Details', it is already implemented in this software and working good, so far.

In case 'refresh_token' need regenerated, through oauth2 setup by manual login to Dropbox and verifying, as mentioned under topic 'Oauth2 Setup' then it automatically saves new 'refresh_token' in database, however it needs to be manually added in code and if we do not want to add in manually, then under topic 'Index.php', some code has been commented in step 6). It can be uncommented to get 'refresh_token' from database automatically. This code is commented, just to keep the work load lower, on this software, because it will make a database call every time to fetch refresh token from there and it can be avoided, at the moment.

If you do not want to try above three solutions, then simply contact software administrator, to find and apply best solution for possible cause of issue.

8) *$baseURL = 'https://your-domain.com/projects/dropbox-to-dropbox/list-and-download.php';*
 header("Location: $baseURL.'?
 access_token=$access_token&&downloading_number=$downloading_number");
 exit;

In this code, we add path of next file to process, that is, 'list-and-download.php' and put it inside a variable '$baseURL'. Later 'header()' function has been used, which is used to send '$access_token', generated at step 7) and '$downloading_number' generated at step 5) and send to file to the file 'list-and-download.php'.

9) *include('footer.php');*
 ?>

At the end of the code 'footer.php' file has been included and PHP tag which were started at top of the page has been closed.

LIST-AND-DOWNLOAD.PHP

This file is linked to mainly downloading 'intro-pictures' folder 't-shirts-pictures' folder from Dropbox to server and enlisting those files, in batches. Following is the code of the file which has been explained below as per steps market. First four steps are linked to getting code from 'header.php' file, verifying logins, collecting required initial static and dynamic variables. From step 5 to 12, 'intro-pictures' are listed and downloaded from Dropbox to server. Step 13 to 25 is linked to enlisting and downloading 't-shirts-pictures' from Dropbox to server. If above steps are complete, then step 26 runs to send 'access_token' and control to next file 'process-and-upload.php' and if above steps are not complete yet, then step 27 runs to perform pending steps again in current file, by refreshing the page after every five seconds. Step 28 includes code of 'footer.php' file.

Algorithm

Step 1: Start

Step 2: Include header file

Step 3: Read cookie user

Step 4: If cookie user is set
      Display Welcome + cookie value
      Else
      Declare baseURL as path to login file
      Redirect to baseURL

Step 5: Declare variables client_id, client_secret, namespace_id, team_user_id, x, y,
      repeated_items

Step 6: Read access_token and downloading number

Step 7: If access_token is set and not empty & downloading_number is set and not empty
      Declare variables access_token and downloading_number
      Else
      Display message1*
      Add button to redirect to homepage
      Stop any further code execution

Step 8: Declare variable curl

Step 9: Run API using curl, access_token, team_user_id, namespace_id to list all files in
      intro-pictures folder on Dropbox.

Step 10: Declare variable response as API response.

Step 11: Declare variable response1 and assign value of variable response in array format.

Step 12: If response1->entries is not empty
      Declare variable array as response1->entries
      Declare variable image_names as empty array
      Repeat
      for each value of array declare in variable names
      if names->name has dot in value
      Declare variable image_names as names->name

Until all names checked

Repeat

for each value of image_names save index in k and name in new_files

Declare variable new_filename as new_files

If file all-files-listed.txt opens in read mode

Declare variable myfile for file opened.

Else

Display message2*

Stop any further execution of code

Declare variable saved_filepaths to read file using myfile

Declare variable data_array to convert data differentiated by | to array from saved_filepaths

if new_filename is in data_array

if new_filename is set and not empty

Declare repeated_items variable as

values of new_filename + |

Repeat

for each value in data_array as saved_files

if new_filename = saved_files or new_file

value do not have dot

Delete from image_names at index k

Until all saved_files checked

Until all new_files checked

Step 13: If image_names is not empty

Declare and initialize variable a as 0

Repeat

for each value of images_names save in file_names

Declare variable name as file_names

If file all-files-listed.txt opens in read mode

Declare variable myfile as opened

Else

Display message2*

Stop any further execution of code

Declare variable txt as name + |

Write txt in file all-files-listed.txt
Close myfile
Declare variable curl, save_file_loc as path of file name in intro-   pictures and fp to open save_file_loc
Run API to download file named name using variables curl, fp,
access_token, team_user_id, and namespace_id
Save API response in variable response.
Close API.
Increment value of a by 1 for each file downloaded
If a = variable downloading_number
Stop Repeat
Until value of a = variable downloading_number
 Else
Initialize variable x as 1

Step 14: Declare variable curl

Step 15: Run API using variables curl, access_token, team_user_id and namespace_id to list all   files in t-shirts-pictures folder

Step 16: Declare variable response as API response.

Step 17: Declare variable response2 and assign value of variable response in array format.

Step 18: If value of response2->entries is not empty
Declare variable array as response2->entries
Declare variable image_names2 as empty array
Repeat
for each value of array declare in variable names
if value of names->name have dot
Save value of names->name in image_names2
Until all names checked
Repeat
for each value in images_names2 at index k and save name in new_files

Declare new_filename as new_files

If all-files-listed.txt can open in read-only mode

Declare variable myfile for file opened

Else

Display message2*

Stop any further execution of code.

Declare variable saved_filepaths as all-files-listed.txt data

Declare variable data_array for names from saved_filepaths   differentiated by |

If new_filename is present in data_array

If new_filename is set and not empty

Declare variable repeated_items as new_filename + |

Repeat

for each value of data_array declare in saved_files

if new_filename = saved_files or new_filename do not include dot

Delete file at index k in image_names2

Until all values of saved_files checked

Until all new_files checked

Step 19: If image_names2 is not empty

Declare variable b as 0

Repeat

for each value of image_names2 declare in file_names

Declare variable name as file_names

If all-files-listed.txt can open in read-only mode

Declare myfile as opened

Else

display message2*

Stop any further execution of code

Declare variable file_data as data of all-files-listed.txt

Declare variable data_array as values of file_data differentiated by |

If name is not present in data_array

If all-files-listed.txt open in append-mode

Declare variable myfile
Else
Display message2*
Stop any further execution of code
Declare variable txt as name + |
Write value of txt in all-files-listed.txt file
Close myfile
Declare variables curl, save_file_loc as path of name in t-shirts-pictures folder and fp to open file at save_file_loc.

Run API using variables curl, fp, access_token, name, team_user_id and namespace_id to download file name from t-shirts-pictures folder on Dropbox.

Declare variable response to save API response.
Close API.
Increment value of b by 1 for each file downloaded
If value of b = variable downloading_number
Stop execution of Repeat
Until value of b = variable downloading_number
Else
Initiate value of y as 1

Step 20: If x = 1 and y = 1
Declare baseURL as path to process-and-upload.php
Redirect to baseURL along with access_token
Stop any further execution of code
 Else
Display message3*
Refresh this page to repeat this algorithm steps
Include footer file

Step 21: Stop

message1*: Access token not found.
message2*: Unable to open file!
message3*: Downloading and enlisting files. Please wait...

Flowchart

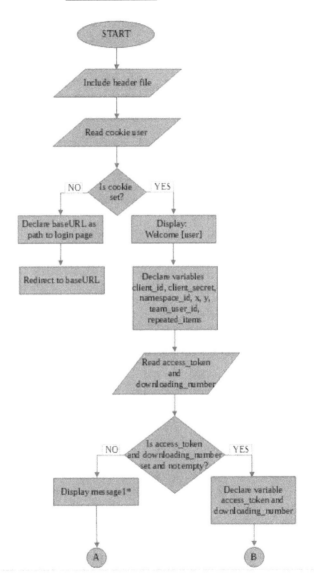

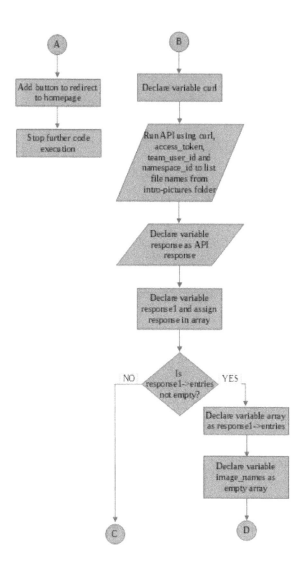

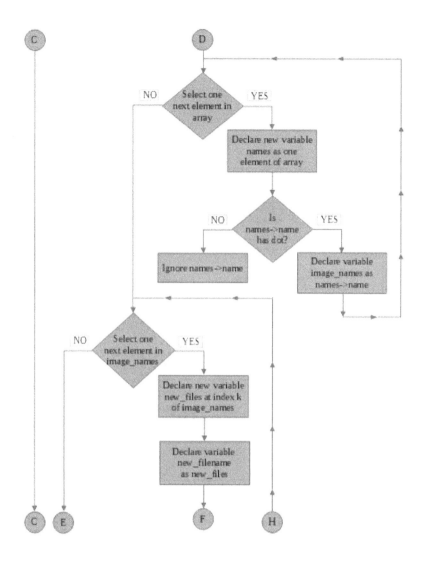

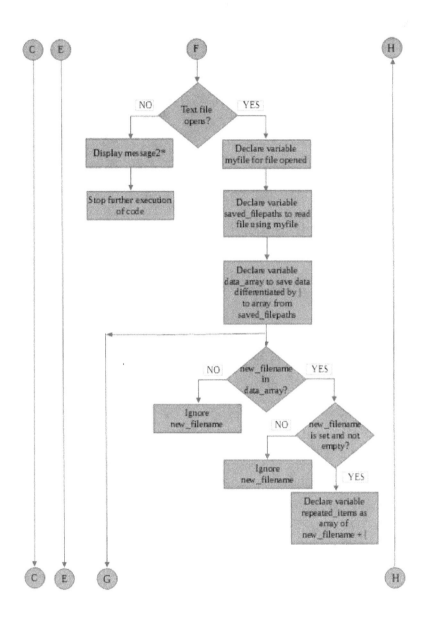

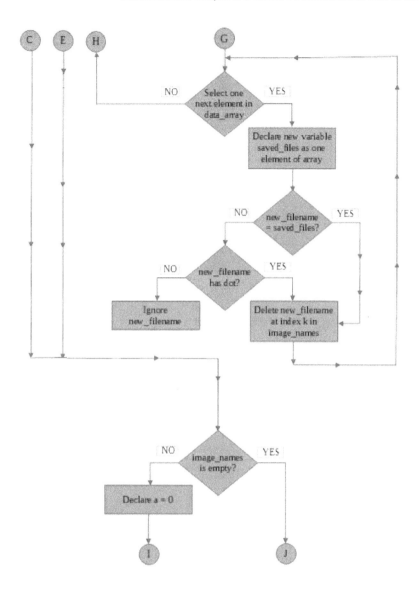

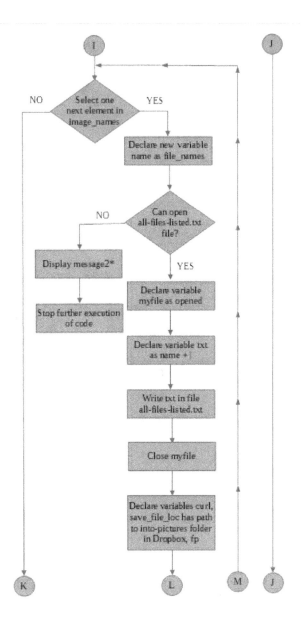

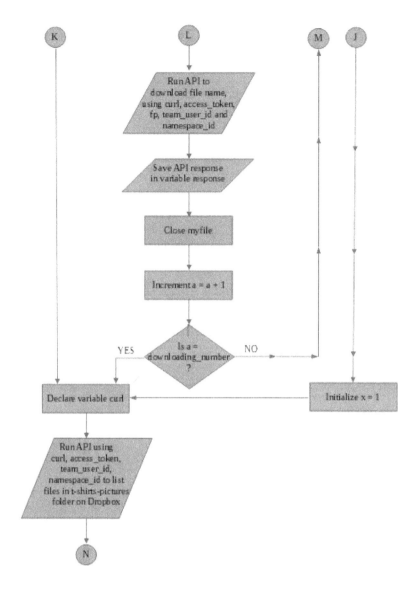

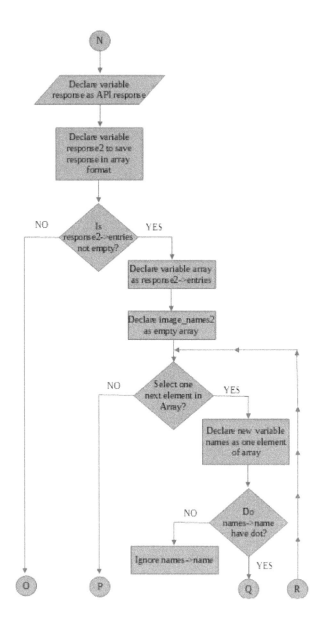

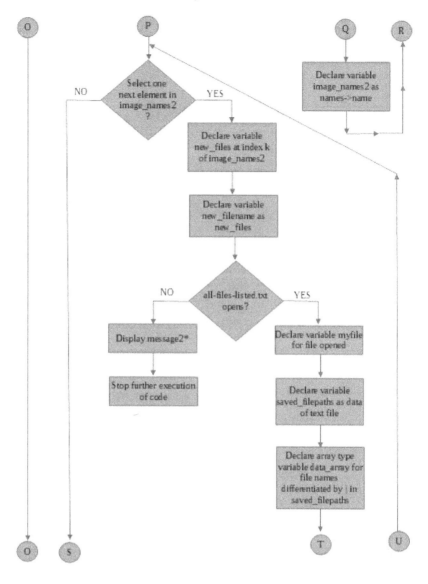

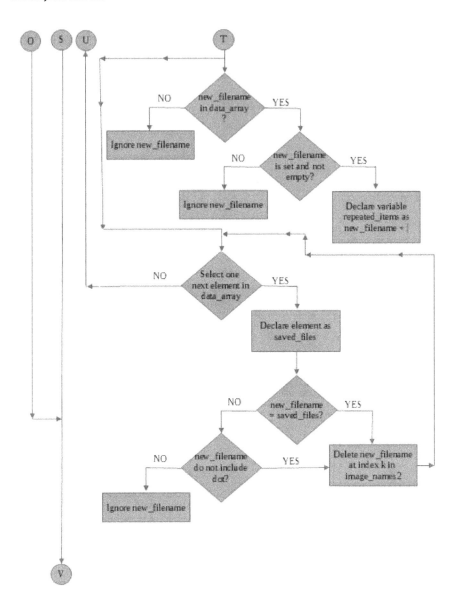

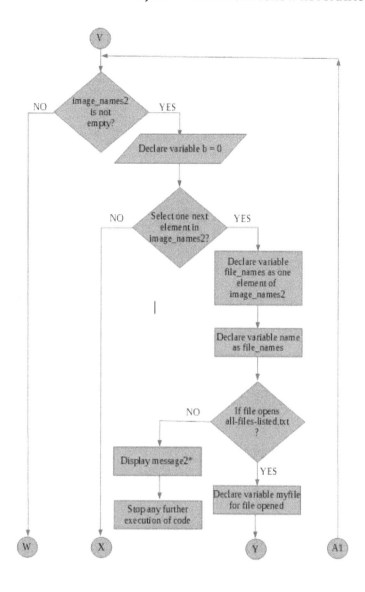

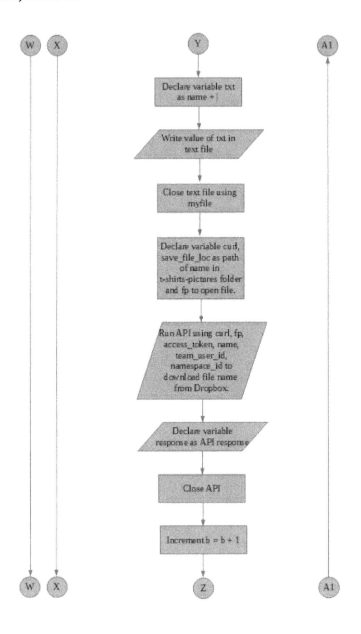

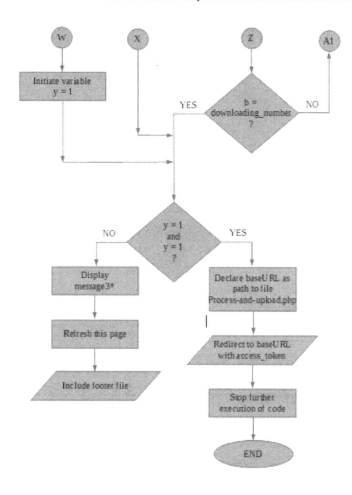

Code

```php
<?php
include('header.php');
```

```
    if(isset($_COOKIE['user'])) {(2)
    echo '<br> Welcome '.$_COOKIE['user'];
  } else {
    $baseURL = 'https://your-domain.com/projects/dropbox-to-
dropbox/login.php';
    header("Location: $baseURL");
  }

    $client_id = "demo_client_id";(3)
  $client_secret = "demo_client_secret";
  $namespace_id = "demo_namespace_id";
  $team_user_id = "demo_team_user_id";
  $x = 0;
  $y = 0;
  $repeated_items = '';


    if(isset($_GET['access_token'])                  &&                  !
empty($_GET['access_token']) &&
      isset($_GET['downloading_number']) &&
      !empty($_GET['downloading_number'])){(4)
    $access_token = $_GET['access_token'];
    $downloading_number = $_GET['downloading_number'];
  } else {
              echo  "<br><br><br><center>Access  token  not
found.<br><br><a
         href='https://your-domain.com/projects/dropbox-to-
dropbox'>
         <button   class='button'>Click   here</button></a></
center>";
    exit;
  }


    $curl = curl_init();(5)
  curl_setopt_array($curl, array(
      CURLOPT_URL => 'https://api.dropboxapi.com/2/files/
```

```
list_folder',
    CURLOPT_RETURNTRANSFER => true,
    CURLOPT_ENCODING => '',
    CURLOPT_MAXREDIRS => 10,
    CURLOPT_TIMEOUT => 0,
    CURLOPT_FOLLOWLOCATION => true,
    CURLOPT_HTTP_VERSION => CURL_HTTP_VERSION_1_1,
    CURLOPT_CUSTOMREQUEST => 'POST',
    CURLOPT_POSTFIELDS
        =>'{"include_deleted":false,"include_has_explicit_shared
_members":
        false,"include_media_info":true,"include_mounted_folde
rs":
        true,"include_non_downloadable_files":false,"path":
        "/Slideshows/intro-pictures","recursive":false}',
    CURLOPT_HTTPHEADER => array(
      'Authorization: Bearer '.$access_token,
      'Content-Type: application/json',
      'Dropbox-API-Select-User: '.$team_user_id,
            'Dropbox-API-Path-Root: {".tag": "namespace_id",
"namespace_id":
        "'.$namespace_id.'"}'
    ),
    ));
    $response = curl_exec($curl);
    curl_close($curl);
    $response1 = json_decode($response, true);


    if(!empty($response1['entries'])){[6]
    $array = $response1['entries'];
    $image_names = array();
    foreach($array as $names){
      if(strpos($names['name'], '.') !== false){
        $image_names[] = $names['name'];
      }
```

```
        }


        foreach($image_names as $k => $new_files){[7]
        $new_filename = $new_files;
        $myfile = fopen("files/all-files-listed.txt", "r") or die("Unable
to open file!");
            $saved_filepaths = fread($myfile,filesize("files/all-files-
listed.txt"));
        $data_array = explode('|', $saved_filepaths);
        if (in_array($new_filename, $data_array)){
            if(isset($new_filename) && !empty($new_filename)){
            $repeated_items .= $new_filename."|";
            }
            }
        foreach($data_array as $saved_files){
        if($new_filename == $saved_files || strpos($new_filename,
".") == false) {
            unset($image_names[$k]);
            }
            }
        }
    }


    if(!empty($image_names)){[3]


        $a = 0;
    foreach($image_names as $file_names){
        $name = $file_names;
        $myfile = fopen("files/all-files-listed.txt", "r") or die("Unable
to open file!");
                $file_data = fread($myfile,filesize("files/all-files-
listed.txt"));
        $data_array = explode('|', $file_data);


        if (!in_array($name, $data_array)){[9]
```

```
        $myfile = fopen("files/all-files-listed.txt", "a") or
die("Unable to open file!");
        $txt = $name.'|';
        fwrite($myfile, $txt);
        fclose($myfile);


        $curl = curl_init();
        $save_file_loc = __DIR__."/files/intro-pictures/".$name;
        $fp = fopen($save_file_loc, 'wb');
        curl_setopt_array($curl, array(
         CURLOPT_URL => 'https://content.dropboxapi.com/2/
files/download',
        CURLOPT_RETURNTRANSFER => true,
        CURLOPT_ENCODING => '',
        CURLOPT_MAXREDIRS => 10,
        CURLOPT_TIMEOUT => 0,
        CURLOPT_FOLLOWLOCATION => true,
                        CURLOPT_HTTP_VERSION   =>
CURL_HTTP_VERSION_1_1,
        CURLOPT_CUSTOMREQUEST => 'POST',
        CURLOPT_RETURNTRANSFER => 1,
           CURLOPT_FILE=> $fp,
        CURLOPT_HTTPHEADER => array(
         'Authorization: Bearer '.$access_token,
                'Dropbox-API-Arg: {"path":"/Slideshows/intro-
pictures/'.$name.'"}',
            'Dropbox-API-Select-User: '.$team_user_id,
                'Dropbox-API-Path-Root: {".tag": "namespace_id",
"namespace_id": "'.
                $namespace_id.'"}'
        ),
        ));
        $response = curl_exec($curl);
        curl_close($curl);
    }
```

```php
      $a++; (11)
    if($a == $downloading_number){
      break;
    }


    }
  } else { (12)
  $x = 1;
}


  $curl = curl_init(); (13)
  curl_setopt_array($curl, array(
      CURLOPT_URL => 'https://api.dropboxapi.com/2/files/
list_folder',
    CURLOPT_RETURNTRANSFER => true,
    CURLOPT_ENCODING => '',
    CURLOPT_MAXREDIRS => 10,
    CURLOPT_TIMEOUT => 0,
    CURLOPT_FOLLOWLOCATION => true,
    CURLOPT_HTTP_VERSION => CURL_HTTP_VERSION_1_1,
    CURLOPT_CUSTOMREQUEST => 'POST',
    CURLOPT_POSTFIELDS
      =>'{"include_deleted":false,"include_has_explicit_shared
_members":
      false,"include_media_info":true,"include_mounted_folde
rs":
      true,"include_non_downloadable_files":false,"path":
      "/Slideshows/t-shirts-pictures","recursive":false}',
    CURLOPT_HTTPHEADER => array(
      'Authorization: Bearer '.$access_token,
      'Content-Type: application/json',
        'Dropbox-API-Select-User: '.$team_user_id,
              'Dropbox-API-Path-Root: {".tag": "namespace_id",
```

```php
"namespace_id": "'.
        $namespace_id.'"}'
  ),
));
$response = curl_exec($curl);
curl_close($curl);
$response2 = json_decode($response, true);


  if(!empty($response2['entries'])){(14)
  $array = $response2['entries'];

    $image_names2 = array();(15)
  foreach($array as $names){
    if(strpos($names['name'], '.') !== false){
      $image_names2[] = $names['name'];
    }
  }

    foreach($image_names2 as $k => $new_files){(16) 17)

      $new_filename = $new_files;


        $myfile  =  fopen("files/all-files-listed.txt",  "r")  or
die("Unable to open file!");(18)
        $saved_filepaths = fread($myfile,filesize("files/all-files-
listed.txt"));
      $data_array = explode('|', $saved_filepaths);


        if (in_array($new_filename, $data_array)){(19)
      if(isset($new_filename) && !empty($new_filename)){
        $repeated_items .= $new_filename."|";
      }
    }
```

```php
        foreach($data_array as $saved_files){(20)
     if($new_filename == $saved_files || strpos($new_filename,
".") == false) {
        unset($image_names2[$k]);
           }
      }
    }
  }


   if(!empty($image_names2)){(21)
   $b = 0;
   foreach($image_names2 as $file_names){
     $name = $file_names;
     $myfile = fopen("files/all-files-listed.txt", "r") or die("Unable
to open file!");
             $file_data = fread($myfile,filesize("files/all-files-
listed.txt"));
       $data_array = explode('|', $file_data);

       if (!in_array($name, $data_array)){(22)
             $myfile = fopen("files/all-files-listed.txt", "a") or
die("Unable to open file!");
        $txt = $name.'|';
           fwrite($myfile, $txt);
           fclose($myfile);


           $curl = curl_init();(23)
       $save_file_loc = __DIR__."/files/t-shirts-pictures/".$name;
      $fp = fopen($save_file_loc, 'wb');
      curl_setopt_array($curl, array(
        CURLOPT_URL => 'https://content.dropboxapi.com/2/
files/download',
        CURLOPT_RETURNTRANSFER => true,
        CURLOPT_ENCODING => '',
```

```php
        CURLOPT_MAXREDIRS => 10,
        CURLOPT_TIMEOUT => 0,

          CURLOPT_FOLLOWLOCATION => true,
                        CURLOPT_HTTP_VERSION =>
CURL_HTTP_VERSION_1_1,
        CURLOPT_CUSTOMREQUEST => 'POST',
        CURLOPT_RETURNTRANSFER => 1,
        CURLOPT_FILE=> $fp,
        CURLOPT_HTTPHEADER => array(
         'Authorization: Bearer '.$access_token,
             'Dropbox-API-Arg: {"path":"/Slideshows/t-shirts-
pictures/'.$name.'"}',
          'Dropbox-API-Select-User: '.$team_user_id,
             'Dropbox-API-Path-Root: {".tag": "namespace_id",
"namespace_id": "'.
                  $namespace_id.'"}'
             ),
       ));
       $response = curl_exec($curl);
       curl_close($curl);
      }


         $b++;
    if($b == $downloading_number){
      break;
    }
  }


  } else {
   $y = 1;
  }


   if($x == 1 && $y == 1){
```

[24)]

[25)]

[26)]

```php
    $baseURL = 'https://your-domain.com/projects/dropbox-to-dropbox/process-and-
        upload.php';
    header("Location: $baseURL.'?access_token=$access_token");
    exit;

    } else {
    echo '<br><br><br><center>Downloading and enlisting files. Please
        wait...</center><br>';
    header("Refresh:5");
    }

    include('footer.php');
    ?>
```

<u>Code Explanation</u>

1) *<?php*
include('header.php');

First of all PHP tags started, and 'header.php' file is included.

2) *if(isset($_COOKIE['user'])) {*
*echo '
 Welcome '.$_COOKIE['user'];*
} else {
$baseURL = 'https://your-domain.com/projects/dropbox-to-dropbox/login.php';
header("Location: $baseURL");
}

In the next step, it is verified if cookie variable is present. If it is active, then display message 'Welcome user' where 'user' display login email stored in cookie variable. If the cookie variable is not set then software redirects to 'login.php' page.

3) *$client_id = "demo_client_id";*
$client_secret = "demo_client_secret";
$namespace_id = "demo_namespace_id";
$team_user_id = "demo_team_user_id";
$x = 0;
$y = 0;
$repeated_items = '';

After that various static variables have been set with certain initial values. While 'client_id' and 'client_secret' received from Dropbox and 'namespace_id' and 'team_user_id' received from other APIs which need not run again to get these values. These variables will be used to run APIs. Other static variables has been initialized which are 'x' as 0, 'y' as 0 and 'repeated_items' as '' empty value.

```
4)        if(isset($_GET['access_token'])        &&        !
empty($_GET['access_token']) &&
    isset($_GET['downloading_number'])        &&        !
empty($_GET['downloading_number'])){
    $access_token = $_GET['access_token'];
    $downloading_number = $_GET['downloading_number'];
  } else {
            echo "<br><br><br><center>Access token not
found.<br><br>
        <a   href='https://your-domain.com/projects/dropbox-
to-dropbox'>
        <button   class='button'>Click   here</button></a></
center>";
    exit;
  }
```

This code checks if 'access_token' and 'downloading_number' is set inside URL, then get their values and store in variables '$access_token' and '$downloading_number'. If they are not set inside URL then show message 'Access token not found.' and show a button to redirect to homepage.

```
5)  $curl = curl_init();
    curl_setopt_array($curl, array(
        CURLOPT_URL => 'https://api.dropboxapi.com/2/files/
list_folder',
    CURLOPT_RETURNTRANSFER => true,
    CURLOPT_ENCODING => '',
    CURLOPT_MAXREDIRS => 10,
    CURLOPT_TIMEOUT => 0,
    CURLOPT_FOLLOWLOCATION => true,
    CURLOPT_HTTP_VERSION => CURL_HTTP_VERSION_1_1,
    CURLOPT_CUSTOMREQUEST => 'POST',
    CURLOPT_POSTFIELDS
        =>'{"include_deleted":false,"include_has_explicit_shared
_members":false,
```

```
"include_media_info":true,"include_mounted_folders":true
        ,"include_non_downloadable_files":false,"path":
        "/Slideshows/intro- pictures","recursive":false}',
    CURLOPT_HTTPHEADER => array(
      'Authorization: Bearer '.$access_token,
      'Content-Type: application/json',
      'Dropbox-API-Select-User: '.$team_user_id,
            'Dropbox-API-Path-Root: {".tag": "namespace_id",
"namespace_id":
        "'.$namespace_id.'"}'
    ),
    ));
    $response = curl_exec($curl);
    curl_close($curl);
    $response1 = json_decode($response, true);
```

This is an API, which consumes various required variables and gets file names from 'intro-pictures' folder in Dropbox and put them inside variable named '$response1'. Following is the response generated for this API,

```
[entries] => Array
  (
    [0] => Array
      (
        [.tag] => file
        [name] => #2222test.png
        [path_lower] => /slideshows/intro-pictures/#2222test.png
        [path_display] => /Slideshows/intro-pictures/#2222Test.png
        [parent_shared_folder_id] => 4709137073
        [id] => id:4IcjgPAmZGsAAAAAAACQ8A
        [client_modified] => 2023-10-18T14:04:54Z
        [server_modified] => 2023-12-11T02:53:07Z
        [rev] => 0160c3308985e220000000118afbab1
        [size] => 31967
        [sharing_info] => Array
          (
            [read_only] =>
            [parent_shared_folder_id] => 4709137073
            [modified_by] => demo_user-
```

117

2b69DBBVg
)
            [is_downloadable] => 1
            [content_hash]   =>
a5074a0450521dd1ef46407faebd8fcee26e5d
)
        [1] => ...
)

[cursor] => AAGrTN8hWac1rly1LEqu7R-sUBGr9T-
    WMFJYM_JRGl6brjIR9GBqDJZtroOMgXjhOvkeShvHnE5t-
    kTM2QJwfZ2MA1gCwQrl9IiyFBnER6dQhOi_uozkFKopA
[has_more] =>

Here this response generated shows only one file details, however this response is longer and shows all the files' data which are inside 'intro-pictures' folder. This response has been cut using '...' and other files not included because of very lengthy response.

In next step, we can get data from this response at '$response1['entries'].

6) *if(!empty($response1['entries'])){*
    $array = $response1['entries'];
    $image_names = array();
    foreach($array as $names){
      if(strpos($names['name'], '.') !== false){
        $image_names[] = $names['name'];
      }
    }
  }

Next, code verifies if '$response1['entries']' variables is empty or not. If it is not empty, then it save all data inside another variable named '$array'.

After that an array type variable has been initialized at variable '$image_names' with values of empty array 'array()'.

After that 'foreach()' condition is runs, which gets each array related to a file name, and put it inside another variable named '$names'. Now, we can see at response generated in step 5), that '[name]' is where file name is present. It can be accessed inside '$names' variable using '$names[name]'.

Next part of code verifies using 'if()' condition that if dot '.' is present in file name at '$names['name'] (because all file names have extension marked after '.' eg: '.png', '.jpeg', etc.) so that any irrelevant data gets ignored. And all those files' names, gets saved in another array type variable '$image_names'. So, after this code, variable '$image_names' will have values like it,

```
$image_names = [0] => #2222test.png
              [1] => #1111test1.png
              [2] => #1111test2.png
              [3] => #2223test.png
              [4] => #2223test2.png
```

```
7) foreach($image_names as $k => $new_files){
    $new_filename = $new_files;
    $myfile = fopen("files/all-files-listed.txt", "r") or die("Unable to open file!");
          $saved_filepaths = fread($myfile,filesize("files/all-files-listed.txt"));
    $data_array = explode('|', $saved_filepaths);
    if (in_array($new_filename, $data_array)){
      if(isset($new_filename) && !empty($new_filename)){
        $repeated_items .= $new_filename."|";
      }
    }
    foreach($data_array as $saved_files){
        if($new_filename == $saved_files || strpos($new_filename, ".") == false) {
          unset($image_names[$k]);
      }
    }
}
```

Next part of code is used to save only those file names in variable '$image_names', which are not saved in text file 'all-files-listed.txt' file. This code can be further sub-divided into sub parts for explanation,

```
foreach($image_names as $k => $new_files){
    $new_filename = $new_files;
```

For each image file name saved in variable '$image_names', where index of a file is saved in '$k' variable and that specific file name can be accessed through variable '$new_files'. That file name is saved in another variable named '$new_filename'.

```
$myfile = fopen("files/all-files-listed.txt", "r") or
die("Unable to open file!");
    $saved_filepaths = fread($myfile,filesize("files/all-files-
listed.txt"));
    $data_array = explode('|', $saved_filepaths);
```

This part of the code accesses 'all-files-listed.txt' text file using 'fopen()' function and using 'r' for read-only mode. If this text file is not found, then it will show error message 'Unable to open file!'. If file is found, then 'fread()' function, reads file placed at path 'files/all-files-listed.txt'. And all the data of file is saved in the form of an array, in another variable named '$data_array'.

```
if (in_array($new_filename, $data_array)){
    if(isset($new_filename) && !empty($new_filename)){
        $repeated_items .= $new_filename."|";
    }
}
```

This part of code checks if file name saved in variable '$new_filename' is present inside variable '$data_array' which is all file names of text file. This code double checks if variable '$new_filename' is set and is not an empty value for some reason. If it is not empty then save those images name inside another array variable '$repeated_items' with a pipe "|" after each file name.

```
foreach($data_array as $saved_files){
```

```
    if($new_filename == $saved_files || strpos($new_filename,
".") == false) {
        unset($image_names[$k]);
    }
}
```

Next sub-part of the code goes through each file name saved in variable '$data_array' and checks if '$new_filename' variable is present inside it. If this variable is present, delete it from array variable '$image_names', at its index position '$k'.

For each file name, this code goes through file 'all-files-listed.txt' and checks if it is present there, if it is found in text file, then remove it from final array it is generating in variable '$image_names'. This array will help later in case of batch processing, to process only those files which are not saved in text file yet.

```
8) if(!empty($image_names)){
    $a = 0;
    foreach($image_names as $file_names){
        $name = $file_names;
        $myfile = fopen("files/all-files-listed.txt", "r") or die("Unable
to open file!");
        $file_data = fread($myfile,filesize("files/all-files-listed.txt"));
        $data_array = explode('|', $file_data);
```

Next part of the code checks if variable '$image_names' is not empty. Then it initializes a variable '$a' with value 0. And for each image name saved in variable '$image_names', save it inside another variable '$name'.

After that it again opens file 'all-files-listed.txt' using 'fopen()' function in 'r' read-only mode and if this file is not present in folder 'files', it displays message 'Unable to open file!'. If the file is present, then it reads files using 'fread()' function and verifies if file has a size using filesize function. Then it gets all file names of file in another variable named '$data_array'. If there are no fnames, then step 9 to 11 are skipped and step 12) runs.

9) *if (!in_array($name, $data_array)){*
   $myfile = fopen("files/all-files-listed.txt", "a") or die("Unable to open file!");
   $txt = $name.'|';
   fwrite($myfile, $txt);
   close($myfile);

Next part of code checks if image name stored in variable '$name' is not present inside '$data_array' variable, then open file 'all-files-listed.txt' in 'a' append mode. If this file is missing or not accessible for some reason, then it will show error 'Unable to open file!'. Next it saves the '$name' variable inside another variable '$txt' with a pipe '|' in end of end, and writes those new image names to file using 'fwrite' function. After that code closes open file using 'fclose()' function. For example, if file name is '#2223test2', then it will be added in end and saved in text file. '1|' is already present in text file.

1|#1111test1|#1111test2|#2222test|#2223test|#2223test2|

In this way, all file names of 'intro-pictures' folder are saved inside text file.

10) *$curl = curl_init();*
   $save_file_loc = __DIR__."/files/intro-pictures/".$name;
   $fp = fopen($save_file_loc, 'wb');
   curl_setopt_array($curl, array(
      CURLOPT_URL => 'https://content.dropboxapi.com/2/files/download',
      CURLOPT_RETURNTRANSFER => true,
      CURLOPT_ENCODING => '',
      CURLOPT_MAXREDIRS => 10,
      CURLOPT_TIMEOUT => 0,
      CURLOPT_FOLLOWLOCATION => true,
      CURLOPT_HTTP_VERSION => CURL_HTTP_VERSION_1_1,

```
CURLOPT_CUSTOMREQUEST => 'POST',
CURLOPT_RETURNTRANSFER => 1,
CURLOPT_FILE=> $fp,
CURLOPT_HTTPHEADER => array(
 'Authorization: Bearer '.$access_token,
     'Dropbox-API-Arg: {"path":"/Slideshows/intro-pictures/'.
$name.'"}',
    'Dropbox-API-Select-User: '.$team_user_id,
            'Dropbox-API-Path-Root: {".tag": "namespace_id",
"namespace_id": "'.
        $namespace_id.'"}'
 ),
));
$response = curl_exec($curl);
curl_close($curl);
```

After that an API has been used to download those image names from 'intro-pictures' folder from Dropbox, which were saved inside '$name' variable in step 8). This API gives a simple response as follows,

1

```
11) $a++;
   if($a == $downloading_number){
     break;
     }
```

For each image downloaded, value of '$a' increments by 1. In case value of variable '$downloading_number' is 15 and after incrementing '$a' variable value reach 15, it breaks the above repeating operation which started in step 8) to step 11).

```
12) } else {
     $x = 1;
     }
```

Next, part of the code is 'else' condition, which is linked to step 8) above. If '$image_names' variable value is empty, then it will set value of a variable '$x' to 1. This value of '$x' will be used later.

13) $curl = curl_init();
     curl_setopt_array($curl, array(
          CURLOPT_URL => 'https://api.dropboxapi.com/2/files/list_folder',
        CURLOPT_RETURNTRANSFER => true,
        CURLOPT_ENCODING => '',
        CURLOPT_MAXREDIRS => 10,
        CURLOPT_TIMEOUT => 0,
        CURLOPT_FOLLOWLOCATION => true,
        CURLOPT_HTTP_VERSION => CURL_HTTP_VERSION_1_1,
        CURLOPT_CUSTOMREQUEST => 'POST',
        CURLOPT_POSTFIELDS
          =>'{"include_deleted":false,"include_has_explicit_shared_members":false,
          "include_media_info":true,"include_mounted_folders":true,
          "include_non_downloadable_files":false,"path":"/Slideshows/t-shirts-
          pictures","recursive":false}',
        CURLOPT_HTTPHEADER => array(
          'Authorization: Bearer '.$access_token,
          'Content-Type: application/json',
          'Dropbox-API-Select-User: '.$team_user_id,
                'Dropbox-API-Path-Root: {".tag": "namespace_id",
"namespace_id": "'.
          $namespace_id.'"}'
      ),
     ));
     $response = curl_exec($curl);
     curl_close($curl);
     $response2 = json_decode($response, true);

After that an API is hit and it is used to list all the files of folder 't-shirts-pictures' present inside Dropbox and put those image names in a variable named '$response2'. Value of '$response' has been converted from JSON to array using 'json_decode()' function and saved in another variable named '$response2'.

```
[entries] => Array
    (
        [0] => Array
            (
                [.tag] => file
                [name] => TshirtPic1.png
                [path_lower] => /slideshows/t-shirts-pictures/
            tshirtpic1.png
                [path_display] => /Slideshows/t-shirts-pictures/
            TShirtPic1.png
                [parent_shared_folder_id] => 4709137073
                [id] => id:4IcjgPAmZGsAAAAAAACQcw
                [client_modified] => 2023-11-29T02:30:47Z
                [server_modified] => 2023-12-11T02:52:43Z
                [rev] => 0160c3307286d3e0000000118afbab1
                [size] => 98844
                [sharing_info] => Array
                    (
                        [read_only] =>
                        [parent_shared_folder_id] => 4709137073
                        [modified_by] => demo_user-
                    2b69DBBVg
                    )

                [is_downloadable] => 1
                [content_hash]                          =>
5f0ee29cc67665488008e3b1d9cf938f6804
            )

        [1] ...

    )

    [cursor]                                            =>
AAFG4Zr9iVwIkL__o3C7wZdIwx7qYX5DCbKoanrr8E0qKjJksA1d8ByjJyO
    0n-Z9N6zf05HP6RF9mo7m239nByzCOn6Qb8NZUUWyhGoJ-
    hBmJu_by01QG5B3DAkamcncH9ZdRR9T9doJLeU8UGkjm3L11H45Zz
```

nIs

hKUdMax2vezsTfXbMYCh_6SkV9rR5L1Vct_VLqL8CQuXEP-
LBq6yP2-
wtRk8JCEVLOM5YyWeiEnkonZUVjuU1vie5UArlg4XFV4lX0MwaarjJ
BA9N4L_
mfONSRrdRJn-tzxFstpUBT3BGksVzxVUdhTuEzO-rCTkyA
[has_more] =>

Above response generated from the API has a lot of file name entries, however above is shown output of only one file, up to '...', where '...' refers to more files data. We can see that all this data is inside [entries], so we will access data inside '$response2['entries']' in next step.

14) *if(!empty($response2['entries'])){*
    $array = $response2['entries'];

After that it is verified if values inside '$response2['entries']' variable is not empty. If it is not empty then put those values in another variable named $array. We will use it in next step.

15) *$image_names2 = array();*
    foreach($array as $names){
    if(strpos($names['name'], '.') !== false){
    $image_names2[] = $names['name'];
    }
    }

After that another empty array type variable '$image_names2' is initialized with empty array value of 'array()'.

Next, 'foreach()' loop works and '$array' variable is used to access each file's data stored in it separately by storing it in temporary variable '$names'. We can see in output generated at step 13) that file name is present in '[name]'. We can use this variable value for each file name using '$names['name'].

[name] => TshirtPic1.png //Data in API in step 13)
    $names['name'] = 'TshirtPic1.png' //Data fetched in code in step 15)

In above code, 'strpos()' function has been used, which verifies if there is dot '.' in variable value at '$names['name'], eg. '.png', '.jpeg', etc., only then get that file name otherwise avoid file name from getting added in next variable '$image_names2'.

After that '$image_names2' variable will have value of all files names, like,

$image_names2 = [0] => TshirtPic1.png
$\qquad\qquad\qquad$ [1] => TshirtPic2.png
$\qquad\qquad\qquad$ [2] => TshirtPic3.png
$\qquad\qquad\qquad$ [3] => TshirtPic4.png
$\qquad\qquad\qquad$ [4] => TshirtPic5.png
$\qquad\qquad\qquad$ [5] => TshirtPic6.png
$\qquad\qquad\qquad$ [6] => TshirtPic7.png
$\qquad\qquad\qquad$ [7] => TshirtPic8.png
$\qquad\qquad\qquad$ [8] => TshirtPic9.png
$\qquad\qquad\qquad$ [9] => TshirtPic10.png

We can see in above demo output that all the redundant data, except file names in 't-shirts-pictures' folder, has been removed.

16) *foreach($image_names2 as $k => $new_files){*
   $new_filename = $new_files;

   $myfile = fopen("files/all-files-listed.txt", "r") or die("Unable to open file!");
   $saved_filepaths = fread($myfile,filesize("files/all-files-listed.txt"));
   $data_array = explode('|', $saved_filepaths);

   if (in_array($new_filename, $data_array)){
   if(isset($new_filename) && !empty($new_filename)){
   $repeated_items .= $new_filename."|";
   }
   }

```
    foreach($data_array as $saved_files){
    if($new_filename == $saved_files || strpos($new_filename,
".") == false) {
      unset($image_names2[$k]);
    }
  }
}
```

After that this code runs, which goes through file name present in variable '$image_names2', which are not saved in text file 'all-files-listed.txt' file. This code can be further sub-divided into sub parts for explanation:

17) foreach($image_names2 as $k => $new_files){
        $new_filename = $new_files;

For each file name present in '$image_names2' array variable, save file in variable '$new_files' and index of that file is '$k'. After that this image name is saved in another variable named '$new_filename'.

18) $myfile = fopen("files/all-files-listed.txt", "r") or die("Unable to open file!");
          $saved_filepaths = fread($myfile,filesize("files/all-files-listed.txt"));
        $data_array = explode('|', $saved_filepaths);

After that file present at 'files/all-files-listed.txt' is opened in read-only mode using 'r', in case that file is missing, then it will show error message 'Unable to open file!'. After that file 'all-files-listed.txt' is read using 'fread' function and size of file is measured using filesize. After that put this data of file in another variable named '$data_array'.

19)   if (in_array($new_filename, $data_array)){
        if(isset($new_filename) && !empty($new_filename)){

```
    $repeated_items .= $new_filename."|";
    }
}
```

In this code, it is verified if '$data_array' variable contains a file name, named '$new_filename'. Then code double verifies for if value inside variable '$new_filename is set and not empty, then put it inside another variable named '$repeated_items', after added pipe '|' in end of file name.

20)
```
foreach($data_array as $saved_files){
    if($new_filename == $saved_files || strpos($new_filename,
".") == false) {
        unset($image_names2[$k]);
    }
}
```

After that this code runs and for each file name saved inside variable '$data_array' it saves each file name in variable '$saved_files'. It then verifies that if values of variable '$new_filename' is same as variable '$saved_files' value, for each file or if that file have '.' dot present in its file name inside variable '$new_filename'. In that case, delete that file name present at index '$k' from variable '$image_names2' as mentioned in step 15) code above.

21)
```
if(!empty($image_names2)){
    $b = 0;
    foreach($image_names2 as $file_names){
    $name = $file_names;
        $myfile = fopen("files/all-files-listed.txt", "r") or
die("Unable to open file!");
            $file_data = fread($myfile,filesize("files/all-files-
listed.txt"));
        $data_array = explode('|', $file_data);
```

After that it is verified that variable '$image_names2' is not empty. If variable '$image_names2' is not empty, then initialize a variable '$b' with value 0. For each file names in '$image_names2', save file names in variable '$name'. After that code opens text file 'all-files-listed.txt' in read-only 'r' mode, using 'fopen' function. If that file is missing then it shows message 'Unable to open file!'. After that 'fread' function reads file whose size is measured using 'filesize' function. If that data is measurable, then after that all the data of file is saved in variable '$data_array' in the form of array, where the data was divided by pipe '|' symbols.

22)   *if (!in_array($name, $data_array)){*
      $myfile = fopen("files/all-files-listed.txt", "a") or die("Unable to open file!");
         $txt = $name.'|';
         fwrite($myfile, $txt);
         fclose($myfile);

After that code verifies if '$name' variable is not preset in '$data_array' variable, then open file 'all-files-listed.txt' using 'fopen' function, in append 'a' mode. If that file is missing, then show error message 'Unable to open file!'. After that value of variable stored in '$name' variable, is combined with pipe symbol '|' and saved in another variable named '$txt'. After that value of variable '$txt' is saved inside file 'all-files-listed.txt' using 'fwrite' function. After that file is closed using 'fclose()' function.

For example, if value of variable $name is 'tshirtpic10', then it gets added in end of file in 'all-files-listed.txt' and data in file is as follows,

1|#1111test1|#1111test2|#2222test|#2223test| #2223test2|tshirtpic1|tshirtpic2| tshirtpic3|tshirtpic4|tshirtpic5|tshirtpic6|tshirtpic7| tshirtpic8|tshirtpic9|tshirtpic10|

23)   *$curl = curl_init();*

```
$save_file_loc = __DIR__."/files/t-shirts-pictures/".$name;
$fp = fopen($save_file_loc, 'wb');
curl_setopt_array($curl, array(
    CURLOPT_URL => 'https://content.dropboxapi.com/2/
files/download',
    CURLOPT_RETURNTRANSFER => true,
    CURLOPT_ENCODING => '',
    CURLOPT_MAXREDIRS => 10,
    CURLOPT_TIMEOUT => 0,
    CURLOPT_FOLLOWLOCATION => true,
                            CURLOPT_HTTP_VERSION   =>
CURL_HTTP_VERSION_1_1,
    CURLOPT_CUSTOMREQUEST => 'POST',
    CURLOPT_RETURNTRANSFER => 1,
    CURLOPT_FILE=> $fp,
        CURLOPT_HTTPHEADER => array(
    'Authorization: Bearer '.$access_token,
            'Dropbox-API-Arg: {"path":"/Slideshows/t-shirts-
pictures/'.$name.'"}',
        'Dropbox-API-Select-User: '.$team_user_id,
            'Dropbox-API-Path-Root: {".tag": "namespace_id",
"namespace_id": "'.
        $namespace_id.'"}'
    ),
));
$response = curl_exec($curl);
curl_close($curl);
```

After that an API is run which downloads all files named in variable '$name' in step 21) from 't-shirts-pictures' folder on Dropbox. API gives a simple response as follows,

```
1
```

```
24)  $b++;
    if($b == $downloading_number){
```

> *break;*
> *}*

After that variable '$b' which was initialized in step 20), it is incremented by 1 every time a file is listed and downloaded from 't-shirts-pictures' folder. Below it a condition is set, so that if variable '$downloading_number' has value 15 and value of variable '$b' after regularly incrementing, reaches value of '$downloading_number' variable then stop executing above part of code and move on to next code in file.

25) *} else {*
    $y = 1;
    }

This 'else' condition is linked to 'if' condition of step 21). This condition will run if variable '$image_names2' is empty, then value of variable '$y' is set to 1.

26) *if($x == 1 && $y == 1){*
    $baseURL = 'https://your-domain.com/projects/dropbox-to-dropbox/process-and-
        upload.php';
    header("Location: $baseURL.'?access_token=$access_token");
    exit;

This part of code checks if value of variables '$x' and '$y' which was set in step 3) to 0. If '$x' is set to 1 in step 12) and value of variable '$y' is set to 1 in step 25), it means that all files has been download, and software redirects the code to next page 'process-and-upload.php' along with value of 'access_token' variable, which was received in step 4).

27) *} else {*
    *echo '

 Downloading and enlisting files. Please*
        *wait...
';*
    header("Refresh:5");

}

In case both '$x' and '$y' is not 1 yet, it means all files from 'intro-pictures' or 't-shirts-pictures' folders not downloaded and then 'else' condition runs. In this case, it shows message on page 'Downloading and enlisting files. Please wait...'. and page is refreshed after a delay of 5 seconds.

Downloading and enlisting files. Please wait...

28) *include('footer.php');*
    ?>

In the end, 'footer.php' file is included and PHP tag is closed using '?>'.

PROCESS-AND-UPLOAD.PHP

This file processes the downloaded image files in 'intro-pictures' folder and 't-shirts-pictures' folder on server which are also enlisted in 'all-files-listed.txt' text file during above topic 'List-and-download.php'.

During this file processing, step 1 to step 8 are used to include 'header.php' file, verify logins, get static and dynamic variables, includes a function and get file paths. Step 9 and 10 are used to verify if there are enough files in 'intro-pictures' and t-shirts-pictures' folder to do further processing of this file. Step 11 to 21 is used to sort out file names, as per requirement for further processing, in case of groups. Step 22 runs, if there are no grouped images (with same numbers). Step 23 selects randomly twelve pictures from 't-shirts-pictures' folder. Step 24 to 28 move selected files from 'intro-pictures' folder and selected files from 't-shirts-pictures' folder and move those files to 'slideshow x' folder on server. Step 29 to 35 are linked to creating zipped file outside 'files' folder from files collected in 'slideshow x' folder. Step 36 to 38 are linked to uploading zip file to Dropbox. After confirming files uploaded successfully, step 39 to 43 delete files on server. After waiting approximately 13 seconds for Dropbox to unzip slideshow, step 44 move unzipped files to 'Slideshows created' folder on Dropbox. Once it is successful, then step 45 to 48 delete zip file and folder in 'slideshow x' folder on Dropbox and display message that slideshow created successfully. This file regularly refreshes after every four seconds to create next slideshows. Step 49 to 59 are used for various kinds of error handling on different steps on Dropbox. Once slideshow created successfully, step 60 moves access to another file, which do further processing.

Algorithm of file 'process-and-upload.php' file has been shown below,

Algorithm

Step 1: Start

Step 2: Include header file.

Step 3: Read cookie user

Step 4: If cookie user is set
  Display message1*
   Else
  Declare variable baseURL as path to login page
  Redirect to baseURL

Step 5: Declare variables client_id, client_secret, namespace_id, team_user_id

Step 6: Declare function searchGroupArrayNumber with variables data and searchVal
  Repeat
  for each value of data at index, save in variable subArray
  For each value of subArray at key, save in value
  If value = searchVal
  Return index
  Return null
   Until all values in data checked

Step 7: If access_token is set and not empty
  Declare variable access_token
   Else
  Display message2*
  Create a button to redirect to homepage

Stop any further execution of code

Step 8: Declare variables intro_pictures_folder as path to intro-pictures folder, t_shirts_pictures_folder as path to t-shirts-pictures folder, slideshow_x_folder as path to slideshow x folder,

Step 9: Declare variable directory_intro_pictures as server directory path to intro-pictures folder

Step 10: Declare variable files_intro_pictures to list files in intro-pictures folder

Step 11: Declare variable total_files_in_intro_pictures_folder and save total number of files in intro-pictures folder

Step 12: Declare variable directory_t_shirt_pictures as server directory path to t-shirts-pictures folder.

Step 13: Declare variable files_t_shirts_pictures to list files of t-shirts-pictures folder.

Step 14: Declare variable total_files_in_t_shirts_folder to save total number of files in t-shirts-pictures folder.

Step 15: If total_files_in_t_shirts_pictures_folder >= 13
      Else
    Display message3*
    Stop any further execution of code
Step 16: If total_files_in_intro_pictures_folder >= 1 &
        total_files_in_t_shirts_pictures_folder >= 13
    Declare variable hideName with values '.', '..' and '.DS_Store'
    Declare variable intro_pictures as empty array type variables
    Repeat
    for each value of files_intro_pictures save in variable filename
    If values of hideName is not in filename
    Display variable intro_pictures as values of filename

Until, all values of files_intro_pictures checked.

Declare variable nums as empty array.

Repeat

for each value of intro_pictures, save in variable intro_pics

Declare variable str with all text removed before #

Declare variable first_letter to get first letter in str   Declare variable nums to delete text from first letter found

Until all values in intro_pictures checked.

Declare variable intro_groups as empty array.

Repeat

for each value of nums counted present at key, save in variable val

If (val > 1)

Declare variable intro_groups as value of key

Until all names in nums checked

If(intro_groups) is set and not empty

Declare variable total_duplicates as total number of values in   intro_groups

Declare variable number as 0

Repeat

value of number = number+1

Declare duplicate_.number as empty array

Repeat

for each value of intro_pictures save in intro_pics

If intro_pics is present in intro_groups[number]

Save   variable   duplicate_.number   as values of intro_pics

Until all values in intro_pictures checked

Until value of number is less than total_duplicates

Declare variable numbe = 0

Repeat

while value of numbe < total_duplicates

Declare variable groups_array as values of

variable duplicate_.numbe

increase value of numbe = numbe + 1

Until numbe = total_duplicates

Declare variable duplicates_unique as empty array.

Repeat

for each value of groups_array, save as inner_array

Declare variable duplicates_unique as first value of inner_array

Until all values of groups_array checked.

Declare variable duplicates_all as all values of groups_array

Declare variable remove_duplicates to list values of intro_pictures which are not in variable duplicates_all

Declare variable added_uniques_intro as all values in remove_duplicates and all values in duplicates_unique

Declare variable intro_picture as first value in added_uniques_intro

Else

Declare variable intro_picture as first value in intro_pictures

Declare variable tshirt_picture as empty array

Repeat

for each value of files_t_shirts_pictures as filename

If values of hideName are not in filename

Declare variable tshirt_picture as filename

Until all files in files_t_shirts_pictures are checked.

Declare variable random_files which have 12 random pictures from tshirt_picture

Declare variable random_tshirt_pictures_array with values from tshirt_picture stored at random_files in locations 0 to 11.

If value of intro_groups is set and not empty

Declare variable uniqueGroupIndex as value received from function

searchGroupArrayNumber($groups_array,

$intro_picture)

If value of uniqueGroupIndex is set

Repeat

for each value of duplicate_.uniqueGroupIndex save in grouped_intro

Declare variable one_group_intro_picture = as path to file name in grouped_intro

Declare   variable   copy_one_group_intro_picture_to as path of   slideshow x folder

Copy   file   grouped_intro   to   slideshow   x   folder

Else

Declare   variable   one_intro_picture   as   path   to intro_picture

Declare   variable   copy_intro_picture_to   as   path   to slideshow

x folder

Copy file intro_picture to slideshow x folder.

Else

Declare   variable   one_intro_picture   as   path   to intro_picture filename   Declare variable copy_intro_picture_to as path to slideshow x folder

Copy file intro_picture to slideshow x folder

Repeat

for each value of random_tshirt_pictures_array save in tshirt_photo

Declare variable one_tshirt_picture as path to file name in   tshirt_photo

Declare   variable   copy_t_shirt_picture_to   as   path to   slideshow x folder

Copy tshirt_photo file to slideshow x folder

Until all files in random_tshirt_pictures_array are copied

Declare variable intro_picture_to_zip to get file name from intro_picture,   without its extension name

Declare   variable   zip_file_name   as   value   stored   in intro_picture_to_zip with .zip added at end of file name.

Declare variable zipArchive to call function ZipArchive

Declare variable zipFile as ./ added in front of zip_file_name

If ZipArchive do not open file zipFile and do not create ZipArchive

Display message4*

Stop any further execution of code

Declare variable folder, as path to slideshow x folder.

Declare function createZip with variables zipArchive and folder

If folder is a directory

If folder can open, declare variable f

Repeat

while directory in f is readable, save in variable file

If file at path folder is a file

If file is not empty and . and ..

Add file to ZipArchive

Else

If file at path folder is directory

If file is not empty and . and ..

Add zipArchive to empty directory at

file, for path folder

Declare folder as

file path

Call function createZip(zipArchive, folder)

Until f is readable

Close f

Else

Display message5*

Stop any further execution of code

Else

Display message6*

Stop any further execution of code

Call function createZip(zipArchive, folder)

Close zipArchive

If zip_file_name exists

Call API using variables curl, zip_file_name, access_token, team_user_id and namespace_id to upload zip file to Dropbox folder at path Slideshows/ slideshow x

Declare variable response to save API response

Close API

Convert response from JSON to array format

Hold execution of code for seven seconds until above tasks   complete

If response[is_downloadable] is not empty

Declare variable folder_name as value of zip_file_name, without .zip

Declare variable from_path as path to slideshow x folder at folder_name

Declare variable to_path as path to Slideshows created folder with folder_name

If intro_groups is set and not empty

If uniqueGroupIndex is set

Repeat

for   each duplicate_.uniqueGroupIndex save as grouped_intro

Delete file grouped_intro in intro-pictures directory

Until all listed files are deleted in duplicate_.uniqueGroupIndex

Else

Delete single file in intro_picture at intro-pictures directory

Else

Delete single file in intro_picture at intro-pictures directory

Declare variable fileList to list all files in slideshow x folder
Repeat
for each value of fileList, save in variable file
If file is verified as a file
Delete file
Until all files in fileList are deleted.
Delete zip_file_name
Hold execution of code for six seconds to wait file
unzipped in Dropbox and for other
processing.
Run API using variables curl, from_path, to_path,
access_token, team_user_id, namespace_id
to move
unzipped files from slideshow x folder to Slideshows
created folder on Dropbox.
Save API response in variable response_move
Close API
Convert value of response_move from JSON to array
format
If response_move[metadata][name] is set and not
empty
Run API using variables curl, zip_file_name,
access_token,   team_user_id   and
namespace_id to delete zip
file on Dropbox
Save API response in variable response
Close API.
Convert value of response from JSON to array
format
Run   API   using   curl,   folder_name,
access_token, team_user_id and
namespace_id   to   delete   folder_name   in
slideshow x folder on Dropbox
Save API response in variable response
Close API

Display message7*

Refresh current page to process next slideshow

Else

Display message8*

Refresh current page to process next slideshow

Else

Display message9*

Declare variable fileList to list all files in slideshow x folder on server.

Repeat

for each value of fileList, save as variable file.

If file is verified as a file

Delete file

Until all files in fileList are deleted.

Delete file zip_file_name on server.

Refresh page to process slideshow again.

Stop any further execution of code.

Else

Display message10*

Declare variable fileList to list all files on slideshow x folder on server

Repeat

for each value of fileList save in variable file.

If file is verified as file

Delete file.

Until all files in fileList are deleted.

Refresh page to process slideshow again.

Stop any further execution of code.

Else

Declare variable fileList to list all files on slideshow x folder on server

Repeat

for each value of fileList, save in variable file

If file is verified as file

Delete file

Until all files listed in fileList deleted.

If text file all-files-listed.txt opens in write mode

Declare variable myfile as opened

Else

Display message11*

Stop any further execution of code.

Write to file myfile as 1| which replace other text in file

Close myfile

Declare variable baseURL as path to file move_files_uploaded.php

Redirect to baseURL and send access_token

Stop any further execution of code.

Step 17: Include footer file

Step 18: Stop

message1*: Welcome {user_email}

message2*: Access token not found.

message3*: Total files in t-shirts-pictures folder are less than 13. Shuffling of 12 images,   need at least 13 t-shirts-pictures. Please add more files.

message4*: Unable to create zip file.

message5*: Unable to open directory folder

message6*: Folder is not a directory.

message7*: Slideshow folder_name created in Dropbox. Please wait...

message8*: One folder folder_name is taking longer to unzip

inside 'slideshow x' folder

on Dropbox. We will try to process it in end of all Slideshows processed.   Please wait...

message9*: Slideshow zip file failed to upload to Dropbox. Please wait, retrying...

message10*: Slideshow zip file not found on hosting server.

message11*: Unable to open file!

Flowchart

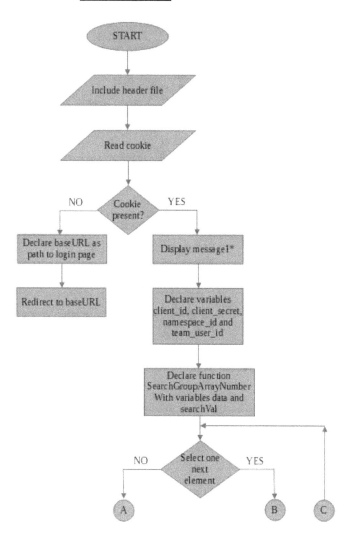

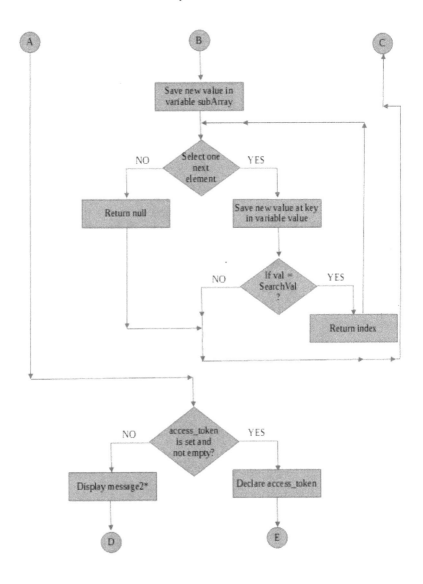

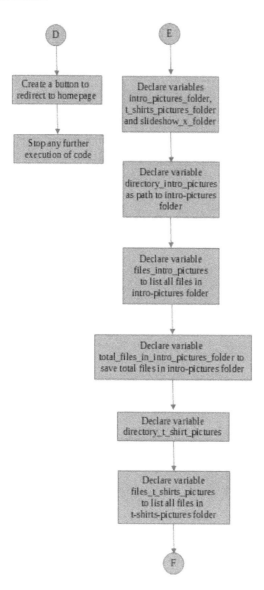

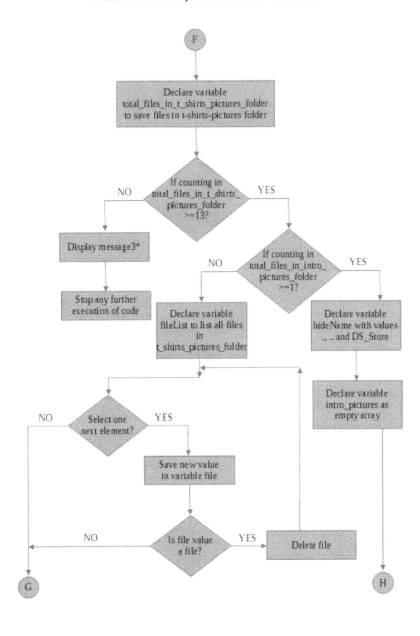

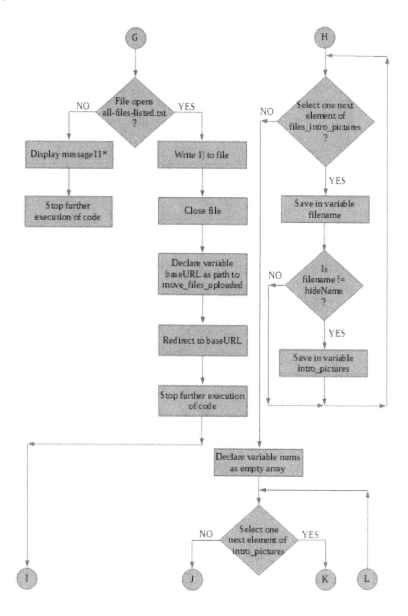

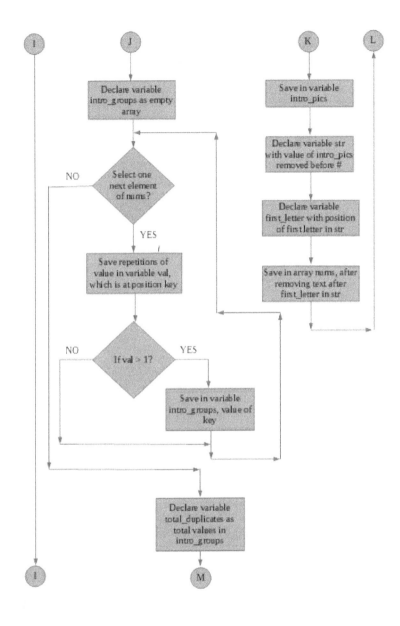

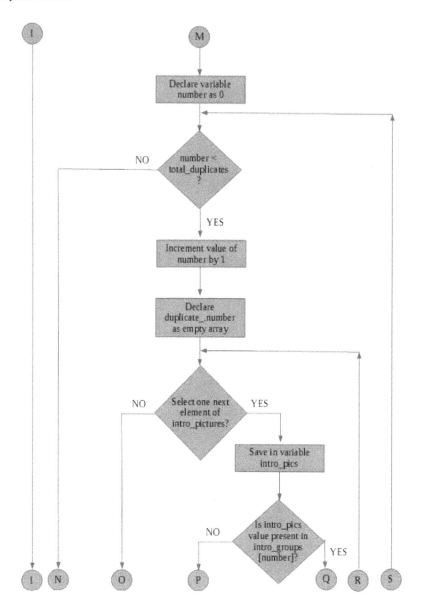

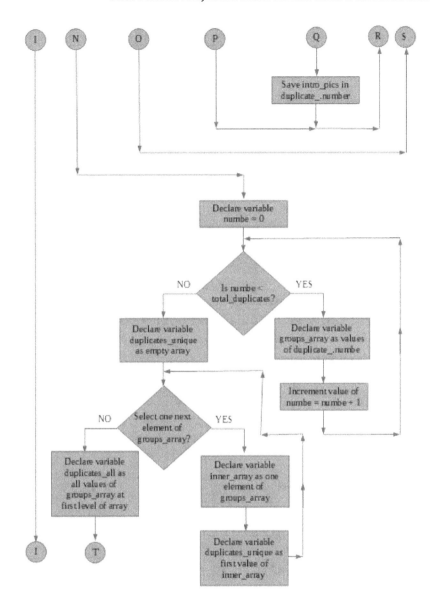

Code

```php
<?php
include('header.php');
```

```php
    if(isset($_COOKIE['user'])) {(2)
    echo '<br> Welcome '.$_COOKIE['user'];
} else {
    $baseURL = 'https://your-domain.com/projects/dropbox-to-
dropbox/login.php';
    header("Location: $baseURL");
}

    $client_id = "demo_client_id";(3)
    $client_secret = "demo_client_secret";
    $namespace_id = "demo_namespace_id";
    $team_user_id = "demo_team_user_id";


    function searchGroupArrayNumber($data,$searchVal){(4)
    foreach($data as $index => $subArray){
       foreach($subArray as $key=>$value){
          if($value === $searchVal)return $index;


            }
    }
    return null;
}

    if(isset($_GET['access_token'])              &&            !
empty($_GET['access_token'])){(5)
    $access_token = $_GET['access_token'];
} else {
    echo "<br><br><br><center>Access token not found.
        <br><br><a   href='https://your-domain.com/projects/
dropbox-to-dropbox'>
        <button    class='button'>Click   here</button></a></
center>";
    exit;
}
```

```php
$intro_pictures_folder = 'files/intro-pictures';
$t_shirts_pictures_folder = 'files/t-shirts-pictures';
$slideshow_x_folder = 'files/slideshow x';


$directory_intro_pictures                =               getcwd()."/".
$intro_pictures_folder;
$files_intro_pictures = scandir($directory_intro_pictures);
$total_files_in_intro_pictures_folder    =
count($files_intro_pictures) - 2;


$directory_t_shirt_pictures              =               getcwd()."/".
$t_shirts_pictures_folder;
$files_t_shirts_pictures = scandir($directory_t_shirt_pictures);
$total_files_in_t_shirts_pictures_folder =
count($files_t_shirts_pictures) - 2;
    if($total_files_in_t_shirts_pictures_folder >= 13){ } else {
    echo "<br><br><br><center>Total files in t-shirts-pictures
folder are less than
        13. Shuffling of 12 images, need at least 13 t-shirts-
pictures. Please add more
        files.</center>";
    exit;
}


if($total_files_in_intro_pictures_folder >= 1 &&
    $total_files_in_t_shirts_pictures_folder >= 13){
$hideName = array('.','..','.DS_Store');


$intro_pictures = array();


foreach($files_intro_pictures as $filename) {
if(!in_array($filename, $hideName)){
$intro_pictures[] .= $filename;
```

```
    }
  }

    $nums = array();12)
  foreach($intro_pictures as $intro_pics){
    $str = strstr($intro_pics, '#');
    $first_letter = preg_replace("/[^a-zA-Z]/", "", $str)[0];
    $nums[] = substr($str, 0, strpos($str, $first_letter));
  }

    $intro_groups = array();13)
  foreach( array_count_values($nums) as $key => $val ) {
    if ( $val > 1 ) $intro_groups[] = $key;
  }

    if(isset($intro_groups) && !empty($intro_groups)){14)

      $total_duplicates = count($intro_groups);15)
    for($number = 0; $number<$total_duplicates; $number++)
{
      ${'duplicate_'.$number} = array();
      foreach($intro_pictures as $intro_pics){
          if (strpos($intro_pics,$intro_groups[$number]) !==
false) {
            ${'duplicate_'.$number}[] = $intro_pics;
              }
        }
      }
    }

      $numbe = 0;16)
    while($numbe < $total_duplicates){
      $groups_array[] = array_merge(${"duplicate_$numbe"});
      $numbe++;
    }

      $duplicates_unique = array();17)
    foreach($groups_array as $inner_array){
      $duplicates_unique[] = $inner_array[0];
```

```
        }

            $duplicates_all = array_merge(...$groups_array); [18]

            $remove_duplicates    =    array_diff($intro_pictures,
$duplicates_all); [19]

            $added_uniques_intro                                   =
array_merge($remove_duplicates,
            $duplicates_unique); [20]


            $intro_picture = $added_uniques_intro[0]; [21]
        } else {

            $intro_picture = $intro_pictures[0];
        }


        $tshirt_picture = array(); [22]
        foreach($files_t_shirts_pictures as $filename) {
          if(!in_array($filename, $hideName)){
            $tshirt_picture[] = $filename;
          }
        }

            $random_files=array_rand($tshirt_picture,12); [23]
                            $random_tshirt_pictures_array    =
array($tshirt_picture[$random_files[0]],
        $tshirt_picture[$random_files[1]],
$tshirt_picture[$random_files[2]],
        $tshirt_picture[$random_files[3]],
$tshirt_picture[$random_files[4]],
        $tshirt_picture[$random_files[5]],
$tshirt_picture[$random_files[6]],
        $tshirt_picture[$random_files[7]],
$tshirt_picture[$random_files[8]],
        $tshirt_picture[$random_files[9]],
```

```php
$tshirt_picture[$random_files[10]],
        $tshirt_picture[$random_files[11]]);


    if(isset($intro_groups) && !empty($intro_groups)) {(24)
                                $uniqueGroupIndex    =
searchGroupArrayNumber($groups_array,
            $intro_picture);

        if(isset($uniqueGroupIndex)){(25)
                foreach(${'duplicate_'.$uniqueGroupIndex} as
$grouped_intro){
                                $one_group_intro_picture  =
$directory_intro_pictures.'/'.$grouped_intro;
                            $copy_one_group_intro_picture_to =
$slideshow_x_folder.'/'.
                $grouped_intro;
                                copy($one_group_intro_picture,
$copy_one_group_intro_picture_to);
        }

        } else {(26)
            $one_intro_picture = $directory_intro_pictures.'/'.
$intro_picture;
                $copy_intro_picture_to = $slideshow_x_folder.'/'.
$intro_picture;
        copy($one_intro_picture, $copy_intro_picture_to);


        }
    } else {(27)
            $one_intro_picture = $directory_intro_pictures.'/'.
$intro_picture;
                $copy_intro_picture_to = $slideshow_x_folder.'/'.
$intro_picture;
        copy($one_intro_picture, $copy_intro_picture_to);
    }
```

```
     foreach($random_tshirt_pictures_array            as
$tshirt_photo){[28]
          $one_tshirt_picture = $directory_t_shirt_pictures.'/'.
$tshirt_photo;
             $copy_t_shirt_picture_to = $slideshow_x_folder.'/'.
$tshirt_photo;
       copy($one_tshirt_picture, $copy_t_shirt_picture_to);
     }

       $intro_picture_to_zip = substr($intro_picture, 0,
         (strlen($intro_picture))-
(strlen(strrchr($intro_picture, '.')))));[29]

       $zip_file_name = $intro_picture_to_zip.".zip";[30]

       $zipArchive = new ZipArchive();[31]
     $zipFile = "./$zip_file_name";
       if ($zipArchive->open($zipFile, ZipArchive::CREATE) !==
TRUE) {
       exit("Unable to create zip file.");
     }

       $folder = 'files/slideshow x/';[32]

       function createZip($zipArchive, $folder)
     {
       if (is_dir($folder)) {
         if ($f = opendir($folder)) {
           while (($file = readdir($f)) !== false) {
             if (is_file($folder . $file)) {
               if ($file != '' && $file != '.' && $file != '..') {
                 $zipArchive->addFile($folder . $file);
               }
                 } else {[33]
               if (is_dir($folder . $file)) {
                 if ($file != '' && $file != '.' && $file != '..') {
```

```
                    $zipArchive->addEmptyDir($folder . $file);
                    $folder = $folder . $file . '/';
                    createZip($zipArchive, $folder);
                  }
                }
                    }
            }
        closedir($f);

            } else {³⁴⁾
        exit("Unable to open directory " . $folder);
      }
          } else {
      exit($folder . " is not a directory.");
    }
  }

    createZip($zipArchive, $folder);³⁵⁾
    $zipArchive->close();

    if( file_exists($zip_file_name)){³⁶⁾

        $curl = curl_init();³⁷⁾
    curl_setopt_array($curl, array(
        CURLOPT_URL => 'https://content.dropboxapi.com/2/
files/upload',
        CURLOPT_RETURNTRANSFER => true,
        CURLOPT_ENCODING => '',
        CURLOPT_MAXREDIRS => 10,
        CURLOPT_TIMEOUT => 0,
        CURLOPT_FOLLOWLOCATION => true,

        CURLOPT_HTTP_VERSION                    =>
CURL_HTTP_VERSION_1_1,
        CURLOPT_CUSTOMREQUEST => 'POST',
                                    CURLOPT_POSTFIELDS   =>
file_get_contents($zip_file_name),
```

```
CURLOPT_HTTPHEADER => array(
    'Authorization: Bearer '.$access_token,
                                    'Dropbox-API-Arg:
{"autorename":false,"mode":"add","mute":false,"path":
        "/Slideshows/slideshow                    x/'.
$zip_file_name.'","strict_conflict":false}',
        'Content-Type: application/octet-stream',
        'Dropbox-API-Select-User: '.$team_user_id,
            'Dropbox-API-Path-Root: {".tag": "namespace_id",
"namespace_id":
            "'.$namespace_id.'"}'
    ),
));
$response = curl_exec($curl);
curl_close($curl);
$response = json_decode($response, true);


    sleep(7);[38)]
    if(!empty($response['is_downloadable'])){

        $folder_name     =    substr($zip_file_name,    0,
strrpos($zip_file_name, ".zip"));[39)]
        $from_path = "/Slideshows/slideshow x/$folder_name/
files/slideshow x";
            $to_path = "/Slideshows/Slideshows created/
$folder_name";


        if(isset($intro_groups) && !empty($intro_groups))
[40)]
        if(isset($uniqueGroupIndex)){
            foreach(${'duplicate_'.$uniqueGroupIndex} as
$grouped_intro){
                unlink($directory_intro_pictures."/".
$grouped_intro);
            }
```

```
        } else {
          unlink($directory_intro_pictures."/".$intro_picture);
        }
      } else {
        unlink($directory_intro_pictures."/".$intro_picture);
      }

        $fileList = glob($slideshow_x_folder . '/*');41)
      foreach ($fileList as $file) {
        if (is_file($file)) {
          unlink($file);
        }
      }


        unlink($zip_file_name);42)


      sleep(6);43)


        $curl = curl_init();44)
      curl_setopt_array($curl, array(
        CURLOPT_URL => 'https://api.dropboxapi.com/2/files/
move_v2',
          CURLOPT_RETURNTRANSFER => true,
          CURLOPT_ENCODING => '',
          CURLOPT_MAXREDIRS => 10,
          CURLOPT_TIMEOUT => 0,
          CURLOPT_FOLLOWLOCATION => true,
                          CURLOPT_HTTP_VERSION   =>
CURL_HTTP_VERSION_1_1,
          CURLOPT_CUSTOMREQUEST => 'POST',
          CURLOPT_POSTFIELDS
                  =>'{"allow_ownership_transfer":true,"allow_sha
red_folder":
                  true,"autorename":true,"from_path":"".
```

```
$from_path."","to_path":
              "".$to_path.""}',
          CURLOPT_HTTPHEADER => array(
          'Authorization: Bearer '.$access_token."",
    'Content-Type: application/json',
    'Dropbox-API-Select-User: '.$team_user_id,
        'Dropbox-API-Path-Root: {".tag": "namespace_id",
"namespace_id":
              "".$namespace_id.""}'
      ),
    ));
        $response_move = curl_exec($curl);
    curl_close($curl);
    $response_move = json_decode($response_move, true);


        if(isset($response_move['metadata']['name']) &&
        !empty($response_move['metadata']['name'])){ [45]


        $curl = curl_init(); [46]
      curl_setopt_array($curl, array(
      CURLOPT_URL =>
              'https://api.dropboxapi.com/2/files/
permanently_delete',
      CURLOPT_RETURNTRANSFER => true,
      CURLOPT_ENCODING => ",
      CURLOPT_MAXREDIRS => 10,
      CURLOPT_TIMEOUT => 0,
      CURLOPT_FOLLOWLOCATION => true,
                    CURLOPT_HTTP_VERSION   =>
CURL_HTTP_VERSION_1_1,
      CURLOPT_CUSTOMREQUEST => 'POST',


        CURLOPT_POSTFIELDS =>'{"path":
        "/Slideshows/slideshow               x/'.
```

```
$zip_file_name.'"}',
        CURLOPT_HTTPHEADER => array(
          'Authorization: Bearer '.$access_token,
          'Content-Type: application/json',
          'Dropbox-API-Select-User: '.$team_user_id,
            'Dropbox-API-Path-Root: {".tag": "namespace_id",
"namespace_id":
                "'.$namespace_id.'"}'
         ),
        ));
        $response = curl_exec($curl);
        curl_close($curl);
        $response = json_decode($response, true);


          $curl = curl_init();[47]
        curl_setopt_array($curl, array(
         CURLOPT_URL =>
                'https://api.dropboxapi.com/2/files/
permanently_delete',
          CURLOPT_RETURNTRANSFER => true,
            CURLOPT_ENCODING => '',
          CURLOPT_MAXREDIRS => 10,
          CURLOPT_TIMEOUT => 0,
          CURLOPT_FOLLOWLOCATION => true,
                    CURLOPT_HTTP_VERSION  =>
CURL_HTTP_VERSION_1_1,
          CURLOPT_CUSTOMREQUEST => 'POST',
              CURLOPT_POSTFIELDS =>'{"path":
              "/Slideshows/slideshow x/'.$folder_name.'"}',
          CURLOPT_HTTPHEADER => array(
          'Authorization: Bearer '.$access_token,
          'Content-Type: application/json',
          'Dropbox-API-Select-User: '.$team_user_id,
            'Dropbox-API-Path-Root: {".tag": "namespace_id",
"namespace_id":
```

```php
                    "'.$namespace_id."'}'
    ),
    ));
    $response = curl_exec($curl);
    curl_close($curl);


            echo      "<br><br><br><center>Slideshow      "'.
$folder_name."' created in
                    Dropbox. Please wait...</center><br>";(48)
    header("Refresh:4");

        } else {(49)

            echo     "<br><br><br><center>One    folder    "'.
$folder_name."' is taking
                    longer to unzip inside 'slideshow x' folder on
Dropbox.</center><br>";
        echo "<br><center>We will try to process it in end of all
slideshows
                    processed. Please wait...</center>";
        header("Refresh:5");
    }

        } else {(50)
        echo "<br><br><br><center>Slideshow zip file failed to
upload to Dropbox.
                    Please wait, retrying...</center>";

        $fileList = glob($slideshow_x_folder . '/*');(51)
    foreach ($fileList as $file) {
      if (is_file($file)) {
        unlink($file);
      }
    }

        unlink($zip_file_name);(52)
        header("Refresh:4");(53)
```

```
      exit;

          }

      } else {(54)
    echo "<br><br><br><center>Slideshow zip file not found on
hosting server.
            </center>";

            $fileList = glob($slideshow_x_folder . '/*');(55)
      foreach ($fileList as $file) {
            if (is_file($file)) {
        unlink($file);
       }
      }

            header("Refresh:4");(56)
      exit;
    }


    } else {(57)
    $fileList = glob($t_shirts_pictures_folder . '/*');(58)
    foreach ($fileList as $file) {
      if (is_file($file)) {
        unlink($file);
          }
    }

      $myfile    =    fopen("files/all-files-listed.txt","w")    or
die("Unable to open file!");(59)
      fwrite($myfile,"1/");
      fclose($myfile);


      $baseURL =
        'https://your-domain.com/projects/dropbox-to-
dropbox/move_files_uploaded.php';(60)
```

```php
    header("Location: $baseURL.'?access_token=$access_token");
    exit;
  }

    include('footer.php');
?>
```

Code Explanation

Following is the details of above code:

1) *<?php*
   include('header.php');

First of all PHP tags started and 'header.php' file is included.

2) *if(isset($_COOKIE['user'])) {*
       *echo '
 Welcome '.$_COOKIE['user'];*
    } else {
       $baseURL = 'https://your-domain.com/projects/dropbox-to-dropbox/login.php';
       header("Location: $baseURL");
    }

This code is part of login page. If cookie is set, then it will display message 'Welcome user', where user is the email of user. In case cookie is not set, then it redirects the page to 'login.php' page immediately and anything of 'process-and-upload.php' page will not show up.

Welcome user_email

3) *$client_id = "demo_client_id";*
   $client_secret = "demo_client_secret";
   $namespace_id = "demo_namespace_id";
   $team_user_id = "demo_team_user_id";

After that static variables are provided to 'process-and-upload.php' page. It includes '$client_id' and '$client_secret' received from Dropbox when app was created earlier. Values of variables '$namespace_id' and '$team_user_id' are extracted from other APIs not useful any more, so not included here.

4) *function searchGroupArrayNumber($data,$searchVal){*
     foreach($data as $index => $subArray){
       foreach($subArray as $key=>$value){
         if($value === $searchVal)return $index;
       }
     }
     return null;
   }

A PHP function named 'searchGroupArrayNumber' has been created. This function will be used later in code at step 24). This function has been created to search a particular index on basis of a value in an particular array type variable. Here '$data' variable is array type variable and '$searchVal' is the value need searched. For example, '$data' variable has following array data,

$data = [0] => [sub-array0] => value1
=> [sub-array1] => value2
[1] => [sub-array0] => value3

First for each value of initial arrays is checked that is [0] and [1] and it is verified if there are sub-array linked to them. If there are sub-array linked to them, as shown in above example [sub-array0], [sub-array1] are sub arrays of [0] and [sub-array0] is sub array of [1]. If sub arrays are present, then this function goes through each of them to check if value stored in variable

'$searchVal' is present is any of sub arrays. For example, if we provide value of '$searchVal' as 'value1', then this function will return first level index of that variable that is [0]. Similarly for 'value2' first level index will be [0] and for 'value3' first level index is [1]. Index could be [0] or [1] in case of above example. We can use that index value for doing certain process, later in the code.

$index = 0 // When $searchVal = 'value1' or 'value2'

$index = 1 // When $searchVal = 'value3'

5)   *if(isset($_GET['access_token'])   &&   !empty($_GET['access_token'])){*
    $access_token = $_GET['access_token'];
    } else {
       *echo   "

 Access   token   not found.

<a*
       href='https://your-domain.com/projects/dropbox-to-dropbox'><button class='button'>Click
       here</button></a> ";
       exit;
    }

Next part of the code, is used to get 'access_token' sent to this page through URL from 'list-and-download.php' file. In this code it is tried to get value of that variable using '$_GET' method and verified if 'access_token' is set using 'isset()' function and not empty, using '!empty()' function and if it is available then save 'access_token' value in another variable '$access_token'. In case if 'access_token' is not set or is empty, then it will show error message 'Access token not found.' and it will show a button named 'Click here' which when pressed then user will be redirected to home page. In case 'access_token' found not set or missing then next part of the code do not run because of 'exit' used below button coding.

6) *$intro_pictures_folder = 'files/intro-pictures';*

$t_shirts_pictures_folder = 'files/t-shirts-pictures';
$slideshow_x_folder = 'files/slideshow x';

Next by using code, paths of folders are set in different variables. In case of 'intro-pictures' folder, its path is stored in variable '$intro_pictures_folder'. Similarly for 't-shirts-pictures' folder, its path is stored in variable '$t_shirts_pictures_folder' and for 'slideshow x' folder, its path is stored in '$slideshow_x_folder'.

7)   *$directory_intro_pictures = getcwd()."/".*
$intro_pictures_folder;
   $files_intro_pictures = scandir($directory_intro_pictures);
            $total_files_in_intro_pictures_folder =
count($files_intro_pictures) - 2;

After that, in case of '$intro_pictures_folder', its actual path on hosting is extracted using 'getcwd()' function and saved in another variable named '$directory_intro_pictures'. Now when we have actual path of folder, then 'scandir()' function is used to list all the files present in 'intro-pictures' folder and saved in variable '$files_intro_pictures'. After that 'count()' function is used to count total number of files in 'intro-pictures' folder. After that two is minus from it and saved in another variable named '$total_files_in_intro_pictures_folder'. We do -2 here because file names included two redundant file names as '.' and '..' and we do not want to count it in names of file.

8)   *$directory_t_shirt_pictures = getcwd()."/".*
$t_shirts_pictures_folder;
   $files_t_shirts_pictures = scandir($directory_t_shirt_pictures);
            $total_files_in_t_shirts_pictures_folder =
count($files_t_shirts_pictures) - 2;

Similarly like step 7), this code works on 't-shirts-pictures' folder. First 'getcwd()' function is used to get actual path of folder on server from visible path stored in variable '$t_shirts_pictures_folder' and it is saved in variable named '$directory_t_shirt_pictures'. After that 'scandir' function is used to scan and get file names of 't-shirts-pictures' folder through the folder's actual path stored in variable '$directory_t_shirt_pictures' and put inside another variable named '$files_t_shirts_pictures'. After that 'count()' function is used to count the total files present in variable '$files_t_shirts_pictures' and subtracted by 2 to remove counting of two non useful file names '.' and '..' getting added by code in variable and this value is stored in another variable named '$total_files_in_t_shirts_pictures_folder'.

9) *if($total_files_in_t_shirts_pictures_folder >= 13){ } else {*

   *echo "

<center>Total files in t-shirts-pictures folder are less than*

   13. Shuffling of 12 images, need at least 13 t-shirts-pictures. Please add more

   files.</center>";

   exit;

   }

Next this code runs and verifies if number of files present in 't-shirts-pictures' folder which is stored inside another variable named '$total_files_in_t_shirts_pictures_folder', if these number of files are '>=' more than or equal to 13, then its all right otherwise 'else' condition runs and displays message 'Total files in t-shirts-pictures folder are less than 13. Shuffling of 12 images, need at least 13 t-shirts-pictures. Please add more files.'. After that 'exit' is run, which don't allow to run any next part of code. It is because later in code there is need of a total of 12 random files which will be selected from 't-shirts-pictures' folder and saved inside each slideshow folder. So, it has been verified if minimum amount of files present to perform this action are present, then proceed, otherwise display message about minimum number of files in 't-shirts-pictures' folder are not present and this condition should be fulfilled first to perform next steps of code.

Total files in t-shirts-pictures folder are less than 13. Shuffling of 12 images, need at least 13 t-shirts-pictures. Please add more files.

10) *if($total_files_in_intro_pictures_folder >= 1 &&*
     $total_files_in_t_shirts_pictures_folder
     >= 13){

It is verified for both folders again that if total number of files in 'intro-pictures' folder which was stored in variable '$total_files_in_intro_pictures_folder' is '>=' greater than or equal to 1 and total files in 't-shirts-pictures' folder stored in variable '$total_files_in_t_shirts_pictures_folder' is greater than or equal to 13, then perform next part of code in step 11). If these conditions are not met, then run step 57).

11)   *$hideName = array('.','..','.DS_Store');*
      $intro_pictures = array();
      foreach($files_intro_pictures as $filename) {
        if(!in_array($filename, $hideName)){
          $intro_pictures[] .= $filename;
        }
      }

In next part of code, we save three values i.e. '.', '..' and '.DS_Store' in a variable named '$hideName'. After that all file names stored in variable '$files_intro_pictures' is checked one by one. From those file names, if there is a file name present such as '.', '..' or '.DS_Store' (where '.DS_Store' file name was found rarely included and can be ignored if found) which are system related names, those names are ignored and rest of the image file names are stored in another variable named '$intro_pictures'. Output of this code looks like as shown below,

$intro_pictures = [0] => #1111test1.png
[1] => #1111test2.png
[2] => #2222test.png

> [3] => #2223test.png
> [4] => #2223test2.png

12) *$nums = array();*
    foreach($intro_pictures as $intro_pics){
      $str = strstr($intro_pics, '#');
      $first_letter = preg_replace("/[^a-zA-Z]/", "", $str)[0];
      $nums[] = substr($str, 0, strpos($str, $first_letter));
    }

In the next part of the code, code goes through each file name present in variable '$intro_pictures' and save each file name in variable '$intro_pics' one by one. Afterwards, in each file name, if there is any text present before '#' it is deleted and result is stored in another variable named '$str'. It is done using function 'strstr()'. For example:

$intro_pics = "It is filename #1111test1.png present.".
'$str' = "#1111test1.png present."

After that it is searched in the variable '$str' that what is the position of first English character in that string. Here function 'preg_replace()' has been used which depend on a 'regex' or 'regular expression' which is a different type of coding language to find patterns in a text.

Regex code = /[^a-z A-Z]/

Here '/' is a delimiter. It represent the start and end of regex. '^' represents start of a string. This code will search for first occurrence of letter in string.

Next 'preg_replace()' function uses pattern provided by regex and search for any values from 'a' to 'z' and 'A' to 'Z'. Following code should output all letters of string,

$str = '#1111test1.png'
preg_replace("/[^a-zA-Z]/", "", $str); // Outputs 'testpng'.
It ignored all numbers

// and special characters '#' and '.'

After that preg_replace code includes '[0]' at end of it, so it will output only one character present at 0th position, as follows,

$first_letter = preg_replace("/[^a-zA-Z]/", "", $str)[0]
$first_letter = t

First English character found 't' is stored in another variable '$first_letter'.

After that, in next line of code, the file name after first 't' in '$str' is removed. Here two functions are used 'strpos()' which gets position before occurrence of variable '$first_letter' in string '$str' and then main function 'substr()' consumes value of this output of 'strpos()' and finds character between 0 and position of first characters in variable '$str'. For example: in above case,

strpos($str, $first_letter) //It gets position of character before first letter 't', that is 4
substr($str, 0, strpos($str, $first_letter) // this code can be written as below,
substr($str, 0, 4) //It gets values of first four characters stored in variable '$str'

$str = "#1111test1.png present."
$nums = "#1111"

In this way '$nums' variable will have only file numbers of each file name. For example, in case of multiple files, in variable '$intro_pictures', as mentioned below,

In case of above example output in step 11), '$nums' variable will have following output,

$nums = [0] => #1111
**   [1] => #1111**
**   [2] => #2222**

> **[3] => #2223**
> **[4] => #2223**

In this way, we get all numbers of image names.

13)   *$intro_groups = array();*
      foreach(array_count_values($nums) as $key => $val) {
        if ($val > 1) $intro_groups[] = $key;
      }

Here first we initialized array name '$intro_groups' as array(). After that inside '$nums' variable, it is counting if a number is present for more than ones or if it is repeated, then using function 'array_count_values()' count number of occurrences of that number. And next, in case, number is present multiple times, it is checked using '$val', if the value in new variable '$val' is more than 1, as used below,

if($val > 1) // If value of $val is greater than '>' 1

In this case, value of variable '$key' in saved inside another variable named '$intro_groups', in the form of array, as follows,
      $intro_groups = [0] => '#1111'
                   [1] => '#2223'

In this way, we get all unique numbers with grouped values.

14) *if(isset($intro_groups) && !empty($intro_groups)){*

After that this code verifies if variable '$intro_groups' is set and not empty. In case this variable is empty, it means there are no groups present and then the 'else' condition of code at step 21) will run. If groups are present, then step 15) runs.

15)   *$total_duplicates = count($intro_groups);*
      for($number = 0; $number<$total_duplicates; $number++)
{
        ${'duplicate_'.$number} = array();
        foreach($intro_pictures as $intro_pics){
          if (strpos($intro_pics,$intro_groups[$number]) !==

false) {

$${'duplicate\_'.\$number}[] = \$intro\_pics;$$

```
            }
        }
    }
```

In this code values of variable '$intro_groups' are counted using 'count()' function and put in another variable named '$total_duplicates'. It is shown in example below,

$total_duplicates = 2 //It include value at [0], [1] in '$intro_groups'

After that a 'for()' loop is run, which has variable named '$number' which starts from 0 and its values increment automatically and will run as many times, as there is numeric value present in variable '$total_duplicates'.

After that an empty variable of type 'array()' is created whose name will be something like 'duplicate_' and after it, current numeric value of '$number' will be added. For example when the loop runs first time, then value of variable '$number' will be 0 and our dynamic variable will have name '$duplicate_0'. When the loop runs second time, then value of variable '$number' will be incremented by one and will 0+1 = 1 and in that case, dynamic variable will have name '$duplicate_1'. Similarly dynamic variable name will keep changing for as many times the loop runs, under the condition explained below.

After that 'foreach()' loop runs, it will search for all file names in variable '$intro_pictures' and temporarily save each image name in another variable named '$intro_pics'. After that following code runs,

if(strpos($intro_pics,$intro_groups[$number]) !== false)

This code compares each value of $intro_groups[$number] as mentioned in 13) with all values in '$intro_pictures' as mentioned in step 12). For example, in case of $intro_groups[number], output is as follows,

$intro_groups[$number] = $intro_groups[0] = '#1111' // When $number = 0
$intro_groups[$number] = $intro_groups[1] = '#2223' // When $number = 1

For each of these two values in example, all the values present in '$intro_pics' will be compared. All values of '$intro_pics' are,

$intro_pics = '#1111test1.png'
= '#1111test2.png'
= '#2222test.png'
= '#2223test.png'
= '#2223test2.png'

Here we can see that when $number = 0, in that case value of '$intro_groups[$number] is '#1111' and following are matches,

#1111test1.png
#1111test2.png

So, the first dynamic variable ${'duplicate_'.$number} generated is,

$duplicate_0 = [0] => '#1111test1.png'
[1] => '#1111test2.png'

When $number = 1, in that case value of '$intro_groups[$number] is '#2223' and following are matches,

#2223test.png
#2223test2.png

In that case, value of second dynamic variable ${'duplicate_'. $number} is,

$duplicate_1 = [0] => '#2223test.png'
[1] => '#2223test2.png'

In this way, we get all image names, of grouped values in separate variables. It will be used later in next step and step 25).

16)   *$numbe = 0;*
       while($numbe < $total_duplicates){
        $groups_array[] = array_merge(${"duplicate_$numbe"});
        $numbe++;
       }

In the next step, a variable '$numbe' is set with initial value of 0. Here 'while' loop is used, it will keep incrementing value of variable '$numbe' one by one by using '$numbe++' mentioned in it, until it is less than value of numeric variable value stored in variable '$total_duplicates'. Here we have value of '$total_duplicates' = 2, as found in step15). So, 'while' loop will run two times, starting from 0, when values is 0 and 1, which is less than 2. When values is 0, code which will run is,

array_merge(${"duplicate_0"})   //dynamic variable 'duplicate_0' called

When value is 1, code which will run is,

array_merge(${"duplicate_1"})   //dynamic variable 'duplicate_1' called

In this process, function 'array_merge()' runs and merge both these arrays 'duplicate_0' and 'duplicate_1', created in step 15), to a new variable value '$groups_array', as shown below,

$groups_array = [0] => [0] => '#1111test1.png'
                     => [1] => '#1111test2.png'
                 [1] => [0] => '#2223test.png'
                     => [1] => '#2223test2.png'

In this way, we get all grouped variables in one variable '$groups_array'. It will be used later in step 24).

17) *$duplicates_unique = array();*
    foreach($groups_array as $inner_array){
     $duplicates_unique[] = $inner_array[0];

}

After that next part of code searches for unique values. For it, it accesses inner array and its 0th position value and put in another variable '$duplicates_unique'. For example, In the above we can see, values at 0th '[0]' position in inner array are following:

> [0] => [0] => '#1111test1.png'
> [1] => [0] => '#2223test.png'

So, in this case of duplicates' unique value, it will have following values,

> $duplicates_unique = [0] => '#1111test1.png'
>   [1] => '#2223test.png'

In this way, we extracted unique values of grouped variables. It will be used in step 20).

18) *$duplicates_all = array_merge(...$groups_array);*

In this code, we merge all the values of variable '$groups_array' from step 16) using 'array_merge()' function and put in one line. For example:

> $duplicates_all = [0] => '#1111test1.png'
>   [1] => '#1111test2.png'
>   [2] => '#2223test.png'
>   [3] => '#2223test2.png'

In this way, we have a normal array with grouped values, which can be used in next step.

19)   *$remove_duplicates = array_diff($intro_pictures, $duplicates_all);*

In next part of code, we remove all the values present in variable '$duplicates_all' from values present in

'\$intro_pictures' using function 'array_diff()'. For example:

$intro_pictures = [0] => #1111test1.png
                  [1] => #1111test2.png
                  [2] => #2222test.png
                  [3] => #2223test.png

                  [4] => #2223test2.png

            - (minus)

$duplicates_all = [0] => '#1111test1.png'
                  [1] => '#1111test2.png'
                  [2] => '#2223test.png'
                  [3] => '#2223test2.png'

            = (equals)

$remove_duplicates = [0] => '#2222test.png'

So, variable '\$remove_duplicates' will have subtracted values. In this way get all non-grouped values.

20) *$added_uniques_intro = array_merge($remove_duplicates, $duplicates_unique);*

In the next part of the code, we merge values of '\$remove_duplicates' from step 19) with values of '\$duplicates_unique' of step 17), using function 'array_merge()' and save in variable '\$added_uniques_intro'. For example:

$remove_duplicates = [0] => '#2222test.png'

            + (plus)

$duplicates_unique = [0] => '#1111test1.png'
                     [1] => '#2223test.png'

            = (equals)

$added_uniques_intro = [0] => '#2222test.png'
                       [1] => '#1111test1.png'

[2] => '#2223test.png'

In the above example, all the values with unique numbers are present. This can be used later in next step and to create unique slideshow names in step 29).

21) *$intro_picture = $added_uniques_intro[0];*
   } else {
   $intro_picture = $intro_pictures[0];
   }

In next part of the code, we select only one picture present at 0th '[0]' position, in case groups of image names with same numbers are present then image selected in that case will be from variable '$added_uniques_intro' that is, '#2222test.png' as shown in step 20).

$intro_picture = #2222test.png

In case if groups of image names with same numbers are not present, then value of '$intro_picture' will be picture name of picture present at 0^{th} '[0]' position, in variable '$intro_pictures' in step 11).

In this step, we have extracted one unique image with unique number from 'intro-pictures' folder, which will be added to new slideshow. In case of group, we will get other images of same number in step 25).

22) *$tshirt_picture = array();*
   foreach($files_t_shirts_pictures as $filename) {
   if(!in_array($filename, $hideName)){
   $tshirt_picture[] = $filename;
      }
   }

In next part of code, code works on variable '$files_t_shirts_pictures' which contain file names of pictures present in 't-shirts-pictures' folder as mentioned in step 8).

Similarly like at step 11), we removed '.', '..' and '.DS_Store' for
't-shirts-pictures' folder in case they are present, by using the
variable '$hideName' created in step 11), then ignore those
file names using function '!in_array()' which represents 'not in
array' in set of files names '$filename' variable created, and
select rest of the file names in a new variable '$tshirt_picture'.
An example has been shown below,

```
$tshirt_picture = [0] => tshirtpic1.png
                  [1] => tshirtpic2.png
                  [2] => tshirtpic3.png
                  [3] => tshirtpic4.png
                  [4] => tshirtpic5.png
                  [5] => tshirtpic6.png
                  [6] => tshirtpic7.png
                  [7] => tshirtpic8.png
                  [8] => tshirtpic9.png
                  [9] => tshirtpic10.png
                  [10] => tshirtpic11.png
                  [11] => tshirtpic12.png
                  [12] => tshirtpic13.png
                  [13] => tshirtpic14.png
                  [14] => tshirtpic15.png
                  [15] => tshirtpic16.png
                  [16] => tshirtpic17.png
                  [18] => tshirtpic19.png
                  [19] => tshirtpic20.png
                  [20] => tshirtpic21.png
                  [21] => tshirtpic22.png
                  [22] => tshirtpic23.png
                  [23] => tshirtpic24.png
                  [24] => tshirtpic25.png
                  [25] => tshirtpic26.png
```

23)   *$random_files=array_rand($tshirt_picture,12);*
                    $random_tshirt_pictures_array   =

array($tshirt_picture[$random_files[0]],
     $tshirt_picture[$random_files[1]],
$tshirt_picture[$random_files[2]],
     $tshirt_picture[$random_files[3]],
$tshirt_picture[$random_files[4]],
     $tshirt_picture[$random_files[5]],
$tshirt_picture[$random_files[6]],
     $tshirt_picture[$random_files[7]],
$tshirt_picture[$random_files[8]],
     $tshirt_picture[$random_files[9]],
$tshirt_picture[$random_files[10]],
     $tshirt_picture[$random_files[11]]);

In above code, we randomly selected 12 file names from '$tshirt_picture' using function 'array_rand()' and put in a variable '$random_files' however this function only get indexes of those file names and not the actual file names. For example, if we have around 40 files in 't-shirts-pictures' folder, 'array_rand()' function get indexes as follows,

    $random_files = [0] => 1
                  [1] => 3
                  [2] => 4
                  [3] => 5
                  [4] => 8
                  [5] => 9
                  [6] => 14
                  [7] => 15
                  [8] => 17
                  [9] => 18
                  [10] => 21
                  [11] => 23

After that these file indexes are put one by one in another variable '$random_tshirt_pictures_array', to get them in a proper structure from the actual array variable '$tshirt_picture', as follows,

$tshirt_picture[$random_files[0]] //this is part of code

We can break above line of code into two parts, as follows,

$random_files[3] = 5 // Here we got index stored at 4th position [3] in

// '$random_files'.

We can put this index in above code, as follows,

$tshirt_picture[5] // It will select the picture name at 6th position [5] in

// '$tshirt_picture' variable in step 22)

'tshirtpic6' // This is output as per step 22)

Value of '$tshirt_picture' variable is received from step 22). As per the above explanation, 12 random image names are selected from 't-shirts-pictures' folder and put in variable '$random_tshirt_pictures_array'. As shown in example below,

$random_tshirt_pictures_array = [0] => 'tshirtpic2'
[1] => 'tshirtpic4'
[2] => 'tshirtpic5'
[3] => 'tshirtpic6'
[4] => 'tshirtpic9'
[5] => 'tshirtpic10'
[6] => 'tshirtpic16'
[7] => 'tshirtpic16'
[8] => 'tshirtpic18'
[9] => 'tshirtpic19'
[10] => 'tshirtpic22'
[11] => 'tshirtpic24'

24)   *if(isset($intro_groups) && !empty($intro_groups)) {*
                                $uniqueGroupIndex =
searchGroupArrayNumber($groups_array,

$intro_picture);

Next we verifies, in case of '$intro_groups' variable, if it is set and not empty, then we run a function 'searchGroupArrayNumber()' as mentioned in step 4). We use it to find the unique index of one selected picture from 'intro-pictures' folder and saved in variable '$intro_picture'. For example, following is structure of '$groups_array' as mentioned in step 16),

$groups_array = [0] => [0] => '#1111test1.png'
=> [1] => '#1111test2.png'
[1] => [0] => '#2223test.png'

=> [1] => '#2223test2.png'

So, in above example, our '$intro_picture' is '#2222test.png' as mentioned in step 21), in that case where this file is not present in '$groups_array', so code will move to step 26). In case the current file we are working on is either '#1111test1.png' or '#1111test2.png, then 0 will be stored in variable '$uniqueGroupIndex'. In case image is '#2223test.png' or '#2223test2.png', then 1 will be stored in variable '$uniqueGroupIndex'. It has been shown in example below,

$uniqueGroupIndex = 0 //If file = '#1111test1.png'
$uniqueGroupIndex = 0 //If file = '#1111test2.png'
$uniqueGroupIndex = 1 //If file = '#2223test.png'
$uniqueGroupIndex = 1 //If file = '#2223test2.png'

25)   *if(isset($uniqueGroupIndex)){*
            foreach(${'duplicate_'.$uniqueGroupIndex} as $grouped_intro){
                    $one_group_intro_picture = $directory_intro_pictures.'/'.$grouped_intro;
                    $copy_one_group_intro_picture_to = $slideshow_x_folder.'/'.
        $grouped_intro;

copy($one_group_intro_picture,
$copy_one_group_intro_picture_to);
    }

Next part of code verifies that if a value is set in variable '$uniqueGroupIndex', then go through all file names, present in dynamic variable which is named similar to 'duplicate_'. In case '$unique_Group_Index' value is 0, then dynamic variable will have name

'$duplicate_0'

and similarly for multiple other numbers. So, in this case, if we check step 15), we created similar variables as '$duplicate_0' and '$duplicate_1' in an example. This code go through file names listed using 'foreach()' loop. For example in '$duplicate_0',

$duplicate_0 = [0] => '#1111test1.png'
[1] => '#1111test2.png'

Variable '$grouped_intro' hold name of each of these files of '$duplicate_0'. Next part of code tries to search these file names inside 'intro-pictures' folder, using variable '$directory_intro_pictures' created at step 7). Similarly, we create a path in 'slideshow x' folder using '$slideshow_x_folder' variable which was created in step 6) and add '$grouped_intro' one file name, in end of it. After that, selected image mentioned in '$grouped_intro' variable, is copied using 'copy()' function from path of image generated for 'intro-pictures' folder where image is present, to 'slideshow x' folder.

26)   *} else {*
    $one_intro_picture = $directory_intro_pictures.'/'.
$intro_picture;
    $copy_intro_picture_to = $slideshow_x_folder.'/'.
$intro_picture;
    copy($one_intro_picture, $copy_intro_picture_to);

```
}
```

In case it is single file, then 'else' condition works. In this case there are no grouped file names, however there could be other grouped file names in whole of 'intro-pictures' folder, in that case, it selects one file name from step 21) selected from step 20) and search its inside 'intro-pictures' folder using variable '$directory_intro_pictures' defined in step 7) and then copy it inside 'slideshow x' folder by selecting its path from variable '$slideshow_x_folder' defined in step 6). 'copy()' function copies file from one folder to another. For example, in step 19), we have such an image,

'#2222test.png'

```
27) } else {
            $one_intro_picture = $directory_intro_pictures.'/'.
$intro_picture;
                $copy_intro_picture_to = $slideshow_x_folder.'/'.
$intro_picture;
         copy($one_intro_picture, $copy_intro_picture_to);
      }
```

In case there are no grouped files present in whole set of 'intro-pictures' folder, as tested in step 24), in that case above code runs which select path of file name present in variable '$intro_picture' get selected at step 21) from step 11) in case of all unique image numbers and its path from variable '$directory_intro_pictures' as defined in step 7) and copy it inside 'slideshow x' folder using variable '$slideshow_x_folder' as mentioned in step 6) using 'copy()' function.

```
28)  foreach($random_tshirt_pictures_array as $tshirt_photo){
            $one_tshirt_picture = $directory_t_shirt_pictures.'/'.
$tshirt_photo;
                $copy_t_shirt_picture_to = $slideshow_x_folder.'/'.
$tshirt_photo;
```

```
copy($one_tshirt_picture, $copy_t_shirt_picture_to);
}
```

In this next code, we go through all files saved in variable '$random_tshirt_pictures_array' as created in step 23) and search path of all these file names in 't-shirts-pictures' directory, by variable '$directory_t_shirt_pictures' created in step 8) and save it using 'copy()' function in 'slideshow_x' folder through variable '$slideshow_x_folder' created in step 6).

29)   *$intro_picture_to_zip = substr($intro_picture, 0, (strlen($intro_picture))-*

(strlen(strrchr($intro_picture, '.')))));

In the next part of code, we select the file name saved in variable '$intro_picture' and try to select its first file name without extension and after last '.' dot, for example, '.png', '.jpeg', etc. must be discarded. For example, we have file name '#1111test1.png', we can apply above code on it and above code can be sub-divided into following sub-parts,

$intro_picture = '#1111test1.png'; //demo file name with 14 character length

strlen($intro_picture) //This code finds length of file name, so gets number 14

strrchr($intro_picture,   '.')   //This   code   finds   the characters after last   //occurrence of dot '.', that is '.png'.

strlen(strrchr($intro_picture, '.')) // This code counts characters including dot and
**   // after last dot, that is 4**

So, the main code becomes:

substr($intro_picture, 0, (14)-(4))

or it can be written as follows,

substr($intro_picture, 0, 10) //This code finds the first 10 characters of variable
//'$intro_picture', that is #1111test1 and removes
//extension completely.

So, variable '$intro_picture_to_zip' have file name, except extension, as follows,

$intro_picture_to_zip = '#1111test1'

30) *$zip_file_name = $intro_picture_to_zip.".zip";*

In next part of the code, we add '.zip', in end of file name generated in variable '$intro_picture_to_zip' and put it inside another variable '$zip_file_name'.

$zip_file_name = '#1111test1.zip'

31)   *$zipArchive = new ZipArchive();*
       $zipFile = "./$zip_file_name";
         if ($zipArchive->open($zipFile, ZipArchive::CREATE) !== TRUE) {
           exit("Unable to create zip file.");
         }

In this code, we call a new function 'ZipArchive()' and save its value in variable '$zipArchive'. Zip file name saved in variable '$zip_file_name', is saved in another variable '$zipFile' after adding './' in front of zip file name. Afterwards, '$zipArchive' tries to create 'ZipArchive with file name saved in variable '$zipFile' using 'ZipArchieve::CREATE'. If it fails to create 'ZipArchive' then software shows error message 'Unable to create zip file.'.

32)   *$folder = 'files/slideshow x/';*
     function createZip($zipArchive, $folder)
     {
          if (is_dir($folder)) {
        if ($f = opendir($folder)) {
          while (($file = readdir($f)) !== false) {
           if (is_file($folder . $file)) {
            if ($file != '' && $file != '.' && $file != '..') {
             $zipArchive->addFile($folder . $file);

                    }
                   }
                  }
                 }
               }
             }

In next part of the code, path of folder 'slideshow x' is stored in variable '$folder'. A function named 'createZip()' has been used. It takes variable value of '$zipArchive' created in step 31) and path of 'slideshow x' folder, where files are present, that is stored in variable '$folder'.

While creating Zip archive, various conditions are checked before adding a file to 'zipArchive()' function. First of all it is verified, if '$folder' is actually a directory using 'is_dir()' function. Then code tries to open folder path using function 'opendir()' and assign this functionality of 'opendir($folder)' in variable '$f'.

After that code tries to repeatedly read files of opened directory using 'readdir()' function, which tries to read '$f'. If code is able to read '$f', then it saves one file name in variable '$file' and will do it repeatedly. After that, another function tries to verify if value stored in variable '$file' is actually a file using 'is_file()' function. If value of variable '$file' is not empty and it is not dot '.' or if it is not double dot '..', then 'zipArchive()' adds the file at path folder, to zip archive using 'addFile()' function. This last paragraph repeats multiple times for each file and adds the files to 'zipArchive()'.

```
33)        } else {
               if (is_dir($folder . $file)) {
                   if ($file != '' && $file != '.' && $file != '..') {
                       $zipArchive->addEmptyDir($folder . $file);
                       $folder = $folder . $file . '/';
                       createZip($zipArchive, $folder);
                   }
               }
           }
       }
       closedir($f);
```

This code works if there is a folder inside 'slideshow x' folder. Code verifies it using 'is_dir()' function. In that case, first code verifies if the folder name, which is saved inside '$file' variable is not empty, if the name has '.' or '..', then it is discarded. Once the folder name is checked, then an empty folder is created inside zipArchive() using 'addEmptyDir()' function. After that zip archive is rebuilt and include all such folder names, if present. In case there are files inside that folder, then they will be worked on using step 32). In the end, closedir($f), closes the directory which was opened in step 32) using 'opendir()' function. Currently this code is running in file outside 'files/slideshow x' folders. So, it also zip these folders. This is why we run an API at step 44) to get files directly inside slideshow folder.

```
34)  } else {
         exit("Unable to open directory " . $folder);
       }
     } else {
       exit($folder . " is not a directory.");
```

```
        }
    }
```

In this code, first 'else' condition is linked to step 32) which runs, if 'opendir()' function fails to open 'files' or 'slideshow x' folder as mentioned in variable '$folder', in that case, it will show error message 'Unable to open directory files/slideshow x'.

Second 'else' condition in this code is linked to 'is_dir()' function of step 32). Code verifies the path provided in '$folder' variable, that is 'files/slideshow x'. In this case if 'files' or 'slideshow x' is not a folder (or directory), then this condition shows error message 'files/slideshow x is not a directory.'

35) *createZip($zipArchive, $folder);*
$zipArchive->close();

Steps listed in 32), 33) and 34) have created a function named 'createZip()', where we can use a variable as created in step 31) '$zipArchive' and a variable '$folder' which has path of 'files/ slideshow x' folder as mentioned in step 32).

In the end, we close the 'zipArchive()' function using 'close()' function. So, no more files can be added to this zip archive.

36) *if(file_exists($zip_file_name)){*

Next part of the code verifies if zip file named '$zip_file_name' has been created and exists using 'file_exists()' function. If it exists then code from step 37) to step 53) runs on basis of various condition checked in next steps. In case this condition is not met, then code will skip rest of step and run step 54).

37)   *$curl = curl_init();*
curl_setopt_array($curl, array(
CURLOPT_URL => 'https://content.dropboxapi.com/2/ *files/upload',*
CURLOPT_RETURNTRANSFER => true,
CURLOPT_ENCODING => '',
CURLOPT_MAXREDIRS => 10,

```
        CURLOPT_TIMEOUT => 0,
     CURLOPT_FOLLOWLOCATION => true,
                    CURLOPT_HTTP_VERSION  =>
CURL_HTTP_VERSION_1_1,
        CURLOPT_CUSTOMREQUEST => 'POST',
                    CURLOPT_POSTFIELDS  =>
file_get_contents($zip_file_name),
      CURLOPT_HTTPHEADER => array(

    'Authorization: Bearer '.$access_token,
                    'Dropbox-API-Arg:
{"autorename":false,"mode":"add","mute":false,"path":
      "/Slideshows/slideshow            x/'.
$zip_file_name.'","strict_conflict":false}',
      'Content-Type: application/octet-stream',
      'Dropbox-API-Select-User: '.$team_user_id,
          'Dropbox-API-Path-Root: {".tag": "namespace_id",
"namespace_id"
          : "'.$namespace_id.'"}'
    ),
    ));
    $response = curl_exec($curl);
    curl_close($curl);
    $response = json_decode($response, true);
```

This API tries to upload one slideshow zip file created to Dropbox's 'slideshow x' folder. It generates a response in variable '$response' in JSON form, this response has been converted to array form, using function 'json_decode()'. It shows following response,

```
[name] => #2222test.zip
[path_lower] => /slideshows/slideshow x/#2222test.zip
[path_display] => /Slideshows/slideshow x/#2222test.zip
[parent_shared_folder_id] => demo-137073
[id] =>demo-ZGsAAAAAAACTjw
[client_modified] => 2023-12-13T21:54:25Z
[server_modified] => 2023-12-13T21:54:25Z
```

```
[rev] => 0160c6b35ec94b90000000118afbab1
[size] => 526062
[sharing_info] => Array
    (
        [read_only] =>
        [parent_shared_folder_id] => id-7073
        [modified_by]           =>           dbid:demo-QvoHyqLEeTzVyX4-
UxnzkdlIWvabnU
    )

[is_downloadable] => 1
[content_hash] => 44b472c0b5ae642d682ab59714a659fc70ccfd7a1df0
```

Once this file uploads, it has this variable '[is_downloadable] => 1'. We can use it in next step. On 'slideshow x' folder on Dropbox, an automation has been set, which automatically unzips the zip file. However unzipped file is currently in raw data form, which includes multiple folders, it includes first the main folder named same as zip file name, inside it is another folder, which is named as 'files', inside it there is another folder named as 'slideshow x' and inside that folder the actual files of that zip file as mention in step 33). So, this need processed further on Dropbox, further processing to fix it will be done at step 44).

38)   *sleep(7);*
         if(!empty($response['is_downloadable'])){

Once the zip file has successfully uploaded in step 37), so the code waits for 7 seconds using 'sleep()' function. Here 'sleep()' function has been set, so that in case past code processed slowly in case of large images' file size and those files are uploaded successfully to Dropbox during these 7 seconds. After these seven seconds complete, software start deleting redundant files which were created on hosting to build and zip a slideshow, so that next slideshow can be created.

After that it is verified ones that the API which is used in step 37) has a response generated which will prove that upload was complete. So, in that case we use '!empty()' function to check if value of API response "$response['is_downloadable']" is not empty then it confirms that upload was successful and code at step 39) runs. In case it is found that response is empty then it will be proved as not successful and then code at step 50) will run.

39)   *$folder_name = substr($zip_file_name, 0, strrpos($zip_file_name, ".zip"));*
           $from_path = "/Slideshows/slideshow x/$folder_name/ files/slideshow x";
                    $to_path = "/Slideshows/Slideshows created/ $folder_name";

After that in variable '$folder_name' we save zip file name and remove its extension '.zip'. It can be divided in multiple steps, as follows,

$zip_file_name = '#2222test.zip' // example zip file name
strrpos($zip_file_name, ".zip") // This code will find the position of .zip i.e. 9
                              // It is at 9th position, because counting from 0
substr($zip_file_name, 0, 9) // This code receives 9 and get first 9 characters
$folder_name = '#2222test'

So, output of above code is #2222test and saved in variable '$folder_name'. After that in another variable '$from_path', we use variable '$folder_name' to create next variable value. It will be like below:

$from_path = '/Slideshows/slideshow x/#2222test/files/ slideshow x'

After that we create another variable named '$to_path' and its value in this demo example will be as follows:
$to_path = '/Slideshows/Slideshows created/#2222test'

These variables will be used later in step 44).

40)   *if(isset($intro_groups) && !empty($intro_groups)){*
         if(isset($uniqueGroupIndex)){
                 foreach(${'duplicate_'.$uniqueGroupIndex} as
$grouped_intro){
                 unlink($directory_intro_pictures."/".
$grouped_intro);
         }
         } else {
            unlink($directory_intro_pictures."/".$intro_picture);
         }
         } else {
            unlink($directory_intro_pictures."/".$intro_picture);
         }

In this part of code, first it is verified that variable '$intro_groups' is set and do not have empty value. In case it is set and not empty, then it is verified that if variable '$uniqueGroupIndex' is set. If the variable '$uniqueGroupIndex' is set, then we will go through the dynamic variable values which is similar to '$duplicate_'. Value of '$UniqueGroupIndex' is added in front of this variable, which could be 0 or 1 in case of demo example or it could be other number on the basis of step 24). Example has been shown below, if '$uniqueGroupIndex' has value is 0 or 1.

'$duplicate_0' // If $uniqueGroupIndex = 0
'$duplicate_1' // If $uniqueGroupIndex = 1

Dynamic variable similar to '$duplicate_' will have data on the basis of step 15). Using 'foreach' loop, we will go through each file name, that is put inside variable '$grouped_intro' and present inside dynamic variable similar to '$duplicate_'. After that add the directory path from variable '$directory_intro_pictures' taken from step 7) and we use 'unlink()' function to delete those files. It deletes all grouped intro pictures from 'intro-pictures' folder with same number.

In case '$uniqueGroupIndex' is not set, then 'else' condition runs and deletes that particular file using 'unlink()' function, by fetching path from variable '$directory_intro_pictures' as set in step 7).

In case variable '$intro_groups' is not set or its value is empty, this refers to there were no groups in whole slideshow and this condition handled separately to delete file using 'unlink()' function on basis of path fetched for variable '$directory_intro_pictures' from step 7).

This code is useful because it removes certain files from 'intro-pictures' folder whose slideshow has been created and we do not want to use those files again in next slideshows. This helps with other code able to automatically select other pending files from 'intro-pictures' folder on basis of group or single file present.

41)   *$fileList = glob($slideshow_x_folder . '/*');*
        foreach ($fileList as $file) {

            if (is_file($file)) {
          unlink($file);
            }
        }

In next code, we try to delete all files in the 'slideshow x' folder on server. First a variable '$fileList' has been created and using 'glob()' function. 'glob()' function selects all files of 'slideshow x' folder on the basis of variable '$slideshow_x_folder' set in step 6) to get path of 'slideshow x' folder on server. After that we go through all files of variable '$fileList' one by one using 'foreach' loop and verifies using 'is_file()' function that if there is a file named as '$file' then delete that file using 'unlink()' function. It deletes all files of 'slideshow x' folder one by one.

42) *unlink($zip_file_name);*

This code deletes using 'unlink()' function, the zip file of slideshow which was created on server.

43)   *sleep(6);*

After that we wait 6 seconds using 'sleep()' function to ensures that all the deletion process is complete successfully and server is ready to process new files for next slideshow in emptied 'slideshow x' folder. It also ensures that in a total wait of 7 seconds in step 38) plus 6 seconds in step 43), Dropbox has successfully unzipped the zip file, using its automated 'unzip' function and we can process on deleting that zip file on Dropbox and do other processes on Dropbox's files and folders.

While it has been observed that sometimes file sizes are even bigger, so slideshow takes longer time to unzip on Dropbox, in that case we will process all pending files under next topic through next file, as mentioned in step 60), however if unzipping file takes even longer, in case of last few zipped slideshows, it is possible, then there is a manual button available in software menu named 'Move files Uploaded', to process those files later.

44)   *$curl = curl_init();*
         curl_setopt_array($curl, array(
         CURLOPT_URL => 'https://api.dropboxapi.com/2/files/
move_v2',
         CURLOPT_RETURNTRANSFER => true,
         CURLOPT_ENCODING => '',
         CURLOPT_MAXREDIRS => 10,
         CURLOPT_TIMEOUT => 0,
         CURLOPT_FOLLOWLOCATION => true,
                        CURLOPT_HTTP_VERSION =>
CURL_HTTP_VERSION_1_1,
         CURLOPT_CUSTOMREQUEST => 'POST',

```
        CURLOPT_POSTFIELDS
          =>'{"allow_ownership_transfer":true,"allow_sha
red_folder":
          true,"autorename":true,"from_path":"'.
$from_path.'","to_path":
          "'.$to_path.'"}',
       CURLOPT_HTTPHEADER => array(
        'Authorization: Bearer '.$access_token.",
        'Content-Type: application/json',
        'Dropbox-API-Select-User: '.$team_user_id,
           'Dropbox-API-Path-Root: {".tag": "namespace_id",
"namespace_id": "'.
            $namespace_id.'"}'
      ),
    ));
    $response_move = curl_exec($curl);
    curl_close($curl);
    $response_move = json_decode($response_move, true);
```

After that we run an API, which selects files from Dropbox at a path mentioned in '$from_path' as created in step 39) and we also gets destination address set in '$to_path' from path created in step 39). We feed these values to this particular API and it create a new folder inside 'Slideshows created' folder on Dropbox, on the basis of file name added in the end of '$to_path' variable. It will have files of slideshow directly inside it, so that they can be accessed easily.

Response of this API has been saved in variable '$response_move' and it has been converted from JSON to array form using 'json_decode()' function. Response of API in array form is shown below,

```
    [metadata] => Array
        (
            [.tag] => folder
            [name] => #2222test
```

```
                [path_lower]    =>    /slideshows/slideshows    created/
#2222test
                [path_display]   =>    /Slideshows/Slideshows   created/
#2222test
                [parent_shared_folder_id] => 4709137073
                [id] => id:demo-GsAAAAAAACTmg
                [sharing_info] => Array
                    (
                        [read_only] =>
                        [parent_shared_folder_id] => 4709137073
                        [traverse_only] =>
                        [no_access] =>
                    )

            )
```

45)   *if(isset($response_move['metadata']['name']) && !*
       empty($response_move['metadata']['name'])){

In next part of code, it is verified that response generated from API in step 44) is positive and have a set and not empty value inside "$response_move['metadata']['name']" then next part of code runs, however sometimes it take even longer for Dropbox automated function to 'unzip' files because of heavy files, so 'else' condition in step 49) will run.

46)   *$curl = curl_init();*
       curl_setopt_array($curl, array(
       CURLOPT_URL =>
              'https://api.dropboxapi.com/2/files/
permanently_delete',
       CURLOPT_RETURNTRANSFER => true,
       CURLOPT_ENCODING => ",
       CURLOPT_MAXREDIRS => 10,

       CURLOPT_TIMEOUT => 0,
       CURLOPT_FOLLOWLOCATION => true,
                     CURLOPT_HTTP_VERSION =>
CURL_HTTP_VERSION_1_1,
       CURLOPT_CUSTOMREQUEST => 'POST',

```
        CURLOPT_POSTFIELDS =>'{"path":"/Slideshows/
slideshow x/'.
            $zip_file_name.'"}',
        CURLOPT_HTTPHEADER => array(
        'Authorization: Bearer '.$access_token,
        'Content-Type: application/json',
        'Dropbox-API-Select-User: '.$team_user_id,
            'Dropbox-API-Path-Root: {".tag": "namespace_id",
"namespace_id": "'.
            $namespace_id.'"}'
        ),
        ));
        $response = curl_exec($curl);
        curl_close($curl);
        $response = json_decode($response, true);
```

If condition at step 45) is successful, then we run an API in step 46). This API deletes latest zip file named '$zip_file_name', as created in step 30), on Dropbox inside 'slideshow x' folder.

```
47)        $curl = curl_init();
        curl_setopt_array($curl, array(
        CURLOPT_URL =>
                'https://api.dropboxapi.com/2/files/
permanently_delete',
        CURLOPT_RETURNTRANSFER => true,

            CURLOPT_ENCODING => '',
        CURLOPT_MAXREDIRS => 10,
        CURLOPT_TIMEOUT => 0,
        CURLOPT_FOLLOWLOCATION => true,
                    CURLOPT_HTTP_VERSION =>
CURL_HTTP_VERSION_1_1,
        CURLOPT_CUSTOMREQUEST => 'POST',
            CURLOPT_POSTFIELDS =>'{"path":"/Slideshows/
slideshow x/'.
```

```
                $folder_name.'"}',
      CURLOPT_HTTPHEADER => array(
      'Authorization: Bearer '.$access_token,
      'Content-Type: application/json',
      'Dropbox-API-Select-User: '.$team_user_id,
          'Dropbox-API-Path-Root: {".tag": "namespace_id",
"namespace_id":
                  '".$namespace_id.'"}'
              ),
      ));
      $response = curl_exec($curl);
      curl_close($curl);
```

After that we run an API which deletes folder named '$zip_file_name', variable value set in step 30), from 'slideshow x' folder present on Dropbox which was set to unzip automatically, as mentioned in step 43).

48)   echo "

 Slideshow '".$folder_name."' created in Dropbox.
         Please wait...
";
      header("Refresh:4");

In case step 45, 46 and 47 are successful, then it shows message for '$folder_name' created at step 39) that "Slideshow '$folder_name' created in Dropbox. Please wait...". After that it refreshes the page after a delay of 4 seconds, so that next slideshow can be created using above steps. Message will show centre aligned in page, as below,

Slideshow '#2222test' created in Dropbox. Please wait...

49)   } else {
      echo "

 One folder '".$folder_name."' is taking
         longer to unzip inside 'slideshow x' folder on Dropbox.
";

*echo "
<center>We will try to process it in end of all slideshows processed.*
    Please wait...</center>";
   header("Refresh:5");
    }

In case step 45) failed because API at step 44) failed to find folder because it was not unzipped on time, because of heavy files, as observed during testing. In that case, it will show message for '$folder_name' created at step 39) that "One folder '$folder_name' is taking longer to unzip inside 'slideshow x' folder on Dropbox. We will try to process it in end of all slideshows processed. Please wait...'. And after that it will refresh the page after 5 seconds, so that next slideshow can be created automatically, on the basis of above steps. An example is shown below,

One folder '#2222test' is taking longer to unzip inside 'slideshow x' folder
We will try to process it in end of all slideshows processed,
Please wait...

50)   *} else {*
     *echo "

<center>Slideshow zip file failed to upload to Dropbox.*
     Please wait, retrying...</center>";
     *echo "

<center>This zip file name may be already present in*
      'slideshow x' folder on Dropbox.</center>";
     $fileList = glob($slideshow_x_folder . '/');*
    foreach ($fileList as $file) {
    if (is_file($file)) {
     unlink($file);
    }
    }

```
    unlink($zip_file_name);
    header("Refresh:4");
    exit;
}
```

In case code at step 38) fails to run, then this 'else' condition runs and it shows error message 'Slideshow zip file failed to upload to Dropbox. Please wait, retrying...'. In this case step 39) to step 49) will not run and when page refresh to create new slideshow again, it will add more images to 'slideshow x' folder and also new zip file, which is not the intended behaviour. So, in the next step, we delete all files from 'slideshow x' folder on server using this code,

Slideshow zip failed to upload to Dropbox. Please wait, retrying...

This zip file name may be already present in 'slideshow x' folder on Dropbox.

51)
```
    $fileList = glob($slideshow_x_folder . '/*');
    foreach ($fileList as $file) {
      if (is_file($file)) {
        unlink($file);
      }
    }
```

This code has been used to in case of condition 50), where variable '$fileList' gets all file names using 'glob()' function from 'slideshow x' folder using variable '$slideshow_x_folder' as generated in step 6). After that 'foreach()' loop has been used to put each file path from variable '$fileList' temporarily into variable '$file'. After that 'is_file()' function has been used to check if file actually exists at that path. After that 'unlink()'

function has been applied on file path variable '$file' which deletes that file from 'slideshow x' folder on server.

In this way, all files gets deleted one by one using above 'foreach()' loop and method used.

52)   *unlink($zip_file_name);*

This code uses zip file name '$zip_file_name' as generated in step 30). After that 'unlink()' function has been applied on zip file to delete the zip file on server.

53)   *header("Refresh:4");*
        exit;

After that 'header()' function has been used which refreshes the 'process-and-upload.php' page after 4 seconds. After that 'exit' has been used to stop any further code of file from running.

So, after page refresh, it will try to add new random files in 'slideshow x' folder again and create new zip file and perform next steps.

54)   *} else {*
    *echo "

<center>Slideshow zip file not found on*
hosting   server.</center>";
        $fileList = glob($slideshow_x_folder . '/');*
      foreach ($fileList as $file) {
      if (is_file($file)) {
        unlink($file);
      }
    }
    header("Refresh:4");
    exit;
  }

In next part of code 'else' condition runs which is linked to step 36). If code verifies that zip file is not found, because of some error, then this 'else' condition will run. It will show error message 'Slideshow zip file not found on hosting server.' After that it will try to delete all images in 'slideshow x' folder on hosting as mentioned in step 55). Error message shows like this,

Slideshow zip file not found on hosting sever.

55)   *$fileList = glob($slideshow_x_folder . '/*');*
           foreach ($fileList as $file) {
              if (is_file($file)) {
                 unlink($file);
              }
           }

This code uses 'glob()' function to get all file names from 'slideshow x' folder using variable '$slideshow_x_folder' which has been created in step 6) and all file names are saved inside variable '$fileList'. After that 'foreach()' loop has been used to temporarily get each file name from '$fileList' variable to '$file' variable. After that it is verified using 'if()' condition and 'is_file()' function that path and file name stored in '$file' variable is actually a file. If it is actually a file, then 'unlink()' function deletes this file using '$file' variable. These steps continue repeatedly until all files deleted in 'slideshow x' folder.

56)   *header("Refresh:4");*
           exit;

After that page has been refreshed using 'header()' function after a delay of 4 seconds. And 'exit' has been used to avoid running any further code of file 'process-and-upload.php', until page refreshes.

After page refreshes, it will try to add new random files in 'slideshow x' folder again and create new zip file to perform next steps.

57) *} else {*
       $fileList = glob($t_shirts_pictures_folder . '/');*
       foreach ($fileList as $file) {

```
        if (is_file($file)) {
        unlink($file);
        }
    }
    $myfile    =    fopen("files/all-files-listed.txt","w")    or
die("Unable to open file!");
        fwrite($myfile,"1|");
    fclose($myfile);
        $baseURL =
        'https://your-domain.com/projects/dropbox-to-dropbox/
move_files_uploaded.php';
        header("Location: $baseURL.'?access_token=$access_token");
        exit;
    }
```

In this 'else' condition is set to run if the 'if()' condition fails to run at step 10). In that case code from Step 11) to 56) will be skipped and this code in 'else' condition will run.

This code is set to run if there are not enough files in 'intro-pictures' folder left or if all slideshows has been created and all pictures deleted one by one (or in groups) from 'intro-pictures' folder. In this particular case, following set of codes run from step 58) to step 60).

```
58)    $fileList = glob($t_shirts_pictures_folder . '/*');
       foreach ($fileList as $file) {
        if (is_file($file)) {
          unlink($file);
        }
       }
```

This code get all file paths at 't-shirts-pictures' folder using 'glob()' function from variable '$t_shirts_pictures_folder' as mentioned in step 8) and save the values in variable '$fileList'. After that 'foreach' loop runs and tries to get files in variable '$file', one by one. For each file it is verified using 'if()' condition and 'is_file()' function that if it is a file actually present there, then delete that file using 'unlink()' function. After deleting all files from 't-shirts-pictures' folder, step 59) runs.

59)   *$myfile   =   fopen("files/all-files-listed.txt","w")   or die("Unable to open file!");*
   fwrite($myfile,"1|");
   fclose($myfile);

This code opens file 'all-files-listed.txt' file using 'fopen()' function in "w" write-mode in 'files' folder. If the code fails to open file, then it run 'die()' function which stops processing of next part of code and shows error 'Unable to open file!'. If file open succeeds, then 'fwrite()' function works and inside file 'all-files-listed.txt' file writes '1|', while the rest of the text gets deleted from file. So, all other file names get deleted from file and replaced with new text '1|'. It has been written because when next set of slideshows will be created and when getting and enlisting slideshow names next time in 'all-files-listed.txt' file, it should not be empty file to add file names to this file. These file names got added to file in topic 'List-and-download.php'. Pipe symbol '|' has been added after 1 because it differentiates different file names in text file 'all-files-listed.txt' file and using this pipe '|' symbol and do not let 1 to add up in some other file name because software will not be able to read incorrect file name from 'all-files-listed.txt' file if it is not named accurately.

60)   *$baseURL =*
   'https://your-domain.com/projects/dropbox-to-dropbox/ move_files_uploaded.php';
   header("Location: $baseURL.'?access_token=$access_token");
   exit;

This code saves the file path 'move_files_uploaded.php' in variable '$baseURL'. After that 'header()' function has been used to move the control to next file named 'move_files_uploaded.php' and along with it 'access_token', which gets sent to file through URL. This 'access_token' was received in this file in step 5). This access token will be used in next file to do various processing in file.

After that 'exit' is used, so next part of code do not need to run, in this particular condition, which started at step 57).

61) *include('footer.php');*
    ?>

This code includes 'footer.php' file in the end of this file's code and closes PHP tag.

MOVE_FILES_UPLOAD ED.PHP

This file is the last file processed in the software operation. This file's code has been divided into three parts. First part of code works if 'access_token' is received from file 'process-and-upload.php' as mentioned in last topic. And in case we press the button in menu 'Move files Uploaded', then second part of code runs, which show only a form with some text and button 'Process pending files' and if this button is pressed, then third part of code runs, which is mostly similar to first part.

Purpose of this file is to finalize software operation, by showing 'Finished creating slideshows.' message and it double checks on Dropbox, if there are pending unzipped folders which failed to process further by 'process-and-upload.php' file, as mentioned in last topic step 49), then process all those unzipped folders and display message for pending folder names processed.

Following is the code of this file, which has been explained below it in steps,

Code

```php
<?php 1)
include('header.php');

if(isset($_COOKIE['user'])) { 2)
    echo '<br> Welcome '.$_COOKIE['user'];
```

```
} else {
    $baseURL       =       'https://your-domain.com/projects/
dropbox-to-dropbox/login.php';
        header("Location: $baseURL");
}

$client_id = "demo_client_id"; (3)
$client_secret = "demo_client_secret";
$namespace_id = "demo_namespace_id";
$team_user_id = "demo_team_user_id";

if(isset($_GET['access_token'])                    &&                    !
empty($_GET['access_token'])){ (4)
    $access_token = $_GET['access_token'];

    $curl = curl_init(); (5)
    curl_setopt_array($curl, array(
        CURLOPT_URL    =>    'https://api.dropboxapi.com/2/
files/list_folder',
        CURLOPT_RETURNTRANSFER => true,
        CURLOPT_ENCODING => '',
        CURLOPT_MAXREDIRS => 10,
        CURLOPT_TIMEOUT => 0,
        CURLOPT_FOLLOWLOCATION => true,
        CURLOPT_HTTP_VERSION                    =>
CURL_HTTP_VERSION_1_1,
        CURLOPT_CUSTOMREQUEST => 'POST',
        CURLOPT_POSTFIELDS
          =>'{"include_deleted":false,"include_has_explicit_shar
ed_members":
          false,"include_media_info":true,"include_mounted_fo
lders":
          true,"include_non_downloadable_files":false,"path"
          :"/Slideshows/slideshow x","recursive":false}',
        CURLOPT_HTTPHEADER => array(
            'Authorization: Bearer '.$access_token.",
            'Content-Type: application/json',
```

```
                'Dropbox-API-Select-User: '.$team_user_id,
                'Dropbox-API-Path-Root: {".tag": "namespace_id",
"namespace_id":
                    "'.$namespace_id.'"}'
        ),
    ));
    $response = curl_exec($curl);
    curl_close($curl);
    $response= json_decode($response, true);

    if(empty($response['entries'])) {⁵⁾
        echo  "<br><br><br><center><h1>Finished  creating
slideshows.
            </h1></center><br>";
        echo "<br><br><br><center><img src='fireworks2.gif'
style='width:20px;'>
            </center></img>";
        exit;
    }

    $names = array();⁷⁾
    foreach($response['entries'] as $getnames){
        if (strpos($getnames['name'], ".") !== false) { } else {
            $names[] = $getnames['name'];
        }
    }

    $unique_names = array_unique($names);⁸⁾

    foreach($unique_names as $folder_name){⁹⁾
        $zip_file_name = $folder_name.'.zip';
        $from_path      =      "/Slideshows/slideshow     x/
$folder_name/files/slideshow x";
        $to_path     =     "/Slideshows/Slideshows    created/
$folder_name";

        $curl = curl_init();¹⁰⁾
        curl_setopt_array($curl, array(
```

```
            CURLOPT_URL  =>  'https://api.dropboxapi.com/2/
files/move_v2',
            CURLOPT_RETURNTRANSFER => true,
            CURLOPT_ENCODING => '',
            CURLOPT_MAXREDIRS => 10,
            CURLOPT_TIMEOUT => 0,
            CURLOPT_FOLLOWLOCATION => true,
            CURLOPT_HTTP_VERSION                        =>
CURL_HTTP_VERSION_1_1,
            CURLOPT_CUSTOMREQUEST => 'POST',
            CURLOPT_POSTFIELDS
              =>'{"allow_ownership_transfer":true,"allow_share
d_folder":
              true,"autorename":true,"from_path":"'.
$from_path.'","to_path":
              "'.$to_path.'"}',
            CURLOPT_HTTPHEADER => array(
              'Authorization: Bearer '.$access_token.'',
              'Content-Type: application/json',
              'Dropbox-API-Select-User: '.$team_user_id,
              'Dropbox-API-Path-Root: {".tag": "namespace_id",
"namespace_id":
                '".$namespace_id.'"}'
            ),
          ));
          $response_move = curl_exec($curl);
          curl_close($curl);
          $response_move = json_decode($response_move, true);

          if(isset($response_move['metadata']['name']) &&
            !empty($response_move['metadata']['name'])){[11]

              $curl = curl_init();[12]
              curl_setopt_array($curl, array(
                CURLOPT_URL =>
                  'https://api.dropboxapi.com/2/files/
```

```
permanently_delete',
            CURLOPT_RETURNTRANSFER => true,
            CURLOPT_ENCODING => '',
            CURLOPT_MAXREDIRS => 10,
            CURLOPT_TIMEOUT => 0,
            CURLOPT_FOLLOWLOCATION => true,
            CURLOPT_HTTP_VERSION                 =>
CURL_HTTP_VERSION_1_1,
            CURLOPT_CUSTOMREQUEST => 'POST',
            CURLOPT_POSTFIELDS =>'{"path":
              "/Slideshows/slideshow x/'.$zip_file_name.'"}',
            CURLOPT_HTTPHEADER => array(
              'Authorization: Bearer '.$access_token,
              'Content-Type: application/json',
              'Dropbox-API-Select-User: '.$team_user_id,
              'Dropbox-API-Path-Root:                 {".tag":
"namespace_id", "namespace_id":
              "'.$namespace_id.'"}'
            ),
          ));
          $response = curl_exec($curl);
          curl_close($curl);
          $response = json_decode($response, true);

          sleep(1); 13)

          $curl = curl_init(); 14)
          curl_setopt_array($curl, array(
            CURLOPT_URL =>
              'https://api.dropboxapi.com/2/files/
permanently_delete',
            CURLOPT_RETURNTRANSFER => true,
            CURLOPT_ENCODING => '',
            CURLOPT_MAXREDIRS => 10,
            CURLOPT_TIMEOUT => 0,
            CURLOPT_FOLLOWLOCATION => true,
```

```
            CURLOPT_HTTP_VERSION                       =>
CURL_HTTP_VERSION_1_1,
            CURLOPT_CUSTOMREQUEST => 'POST',
            CURLOPT_POSTFIELDS =>'{"path":
            "/Slideshows/slideshow x/'.$folder_name.'"}',
            CURLOPT_HTTPHEADER => array(
            'Authorization: Bearer '.$access_token,
            'Content-Type: application/json',
            'Dropbox-API-Select-User: '.$team_user_id,
            'Dropbox-API-Path-Root:                    {".tag":
"namespace_id", "namespace_id":
                "'.$namespace_id.'"}'
            ),
            ));
            $response = curl_exec($curl);
            curl_close($curl);
        }

        echo  "<br><div  style='padding-left:50px;  padding-
right:50px;'>
            <center>Processed   pending   '".$folder_name."'   in
'slideshow x' folder on
            Dropbox.</center></div><br>";[15]
        }

        echo    "<br><br><br><center><h1>Finished    creating
slideshows.
            </h1></center><br>";[16]
        echo  "<br><br><br><center><img  src='fireworks2.gif'
style='width:20px;'>
            </center></img>";
        exit;
    } else {[17]
        echo "<br><br><br><center>Moves files from 'slideshow
x' folder to 'Slideshows
            created' folder. </center>";
```

*echo "

 *

It is observed that sometimes because of heavy files Dropbox's automated

'unzip' function takes longer in 'slideshow x' folder on Dropbox and some

operations not performed because of this reason. In this case, files are still

present in 'slideshow x' folder and for further processing, this page can be used

to complete pending tasks, in series, for all unzipped slideshows at ones, by

below button. ";

if(isset($_POST['do']) && !empty($_POST['do'])){[19]

$refresh_token =
"demo_refresh_token-
OL",[20]

$curl = curl_init();[21]
curl_setopt_array($curl, array(
CURLOPT_URL   =>   'https://api.dropbox.com/oauth2/token',
CURLOPT_RETURNTRANSFER => true,
CURLOPT_ENCODING => ",
CURLOPT_MAXREDIRS => 10,
CURLOPT_TIMEOUT => 0,
CURLOPT_FOLLOWLOCATION => true,
CURLOPT_HTTP_VERSION   =>
CURL_HTTP_VERSION_1_1,
CURLOPT_CUSTOMREQUEST => 'POST',
CURLOPT_POSTFIELDS   =>
'grant_type=refresh_token&refresh_token=
'.$refresh_token.'&client_id='.
$client_id.'&client_secret='.$client_secret.",
CURLOPT_HTTPHEADER => array(

```
            'Content-Type:              application/x-www-form-
urlencoded'
        ),
    ));
    $response = curl_exec($curl);
    curl_close($curl);
    $response = json_decode($response, true);

    if(!empty($response['access_token'])){(22)
        $access_token = $response['access_token'];
    } else {
        echo "Dropbox Access Token missing. It could be
because of temporary
            network error, refresh token may've expired, etc.
Please retry after some
            time or contact this software administrator.";
        exit;
    }

    $curl = curl_init();(23)
    curl_setopt_array($curl, array(
        CURLOPT_URL  =>  'https://api.dropboxapi.com/2/
files/list_folder',
        CURLOPT_RETURNTRANSFER => true,
        CURLOPT_ENCODING => ",
        CURLOPT_MAXREDIRS => 10,
        CURLOPT_TIMEOUT => 0,
        CURLOPT_FOLLOWLOCATION => true,
        CURLOPT_HTTP_VERSION                          =>
CURL_HTTP_VERSION_1_1,
        CURLOPT_CUSTOMREQUEST => 'POST',
        CURLOPT_POSTFIELDS
        =>'{"include_deleted":false,"include_has_explicit_s
hared_members":
            false,"include_media_info":true,"include_mounted
_folders":
```

```
                    true,"include_non_downloadable_files":false,"path"
:
                    "/Slideshows/slideshow x","recursive":false}',
                CURLOPT_HTTPHEADER => array(
                    'Authorization: Bearer '.$access_token.'",
                    'Content-Type: application/json',
                    'Dropbox-API-Select-User: '.$team_user_id,
                    'Dropbox-API-Path-Root:              {".tag":
"namespace_id", "namespace_id":
                        "'.$namespace_id.'"}'
                ),
            ));
            $response = curl_exec($curl);
            curl_close($curl);
            $response= json_decode($response, true);

            if(empty($response['entries'])) {⁽²⁴⁾
                echo '<br><center>No pending files to process.</
center>';
                exit;
            }

            $names = array();⁽²⁵⁾
            foreach($response['entries'] as $getnames){
                if (strpos($getnames['name'], ".") !== false) { } else {
                    $names[] = $getnames['name'];
                }
            }

            $unique_names = array_unique($names);⁽²⁶⁾

            foreach($unique_names as $folder_name){⁽²⁷⁾
                $zip_file_name = $folder_name.'.zip';
                $from_path     =     "/Slideshows/slideshow     x/
$folder_name/files/slideshow x";
                $to_path   =   "/Slideshows/Slideshows   created/
$folder_name";
```

```
$curl = curl_init(); [28]
curl_setopt_array($curl, array(
    CURLOPT_URL                    =>           'https://
api.dropboxapi.com/2/files/move_v2',
    CURLOPT_RETURNTRANSFER => true,
    CURLOPT_ENCODING => '',
    CURLOPT_MAXREDIRS => 10,
    CURLOPT_TIMEOUT => 0,
    CURLOPT_FOLLOWLOCATION => true,
    CURLOPT_HTTP_VERSION               =>
CURL_HTTP_VERSION_1_1,
    CURLOPT_CUSTOMREQUEST => 'POST',
    CURLOPT_POSTFIELDS
    =>'{"allow_ownership_transfer":true,"allow_sha
red_folder":
    true,"autorename":true,"from_path":"'.
$from_path.'","to_path":
    "'.$to_path.'"}',
    CURLOPT_HTTPHEADER => array(
    'Authorization: Bearer '.$access_token.'',
    'Content-Type: application/json',
    'Dropbox-API-Select-User: '.$team_user_id,
    'Dropbox-API-Path-Root:                {".tag":
"namespace_id", "namespace_id":
        "'.$namespace_id.'"}'
    ),
));
$response_move = curl_exec($curl);
curl_close($curl);
$response_move    =   json_decode($response_move,
true);

if(isset($response_move['metadata']['name']) &&
  !empty($response_move['metadata']['name'])){ [29]

    $curl = curl_init(); [30]
```

```
curl_setopt_array($curl, array(
  CURLOPT_URL =>
    'https://api.dropboxapi.com/2/files/
permanently_delete',
  CURLOPT_RETURNTRANSFER => true,
  CURLOPT_ENCODING => '',
  CURLOPT_MAXREDIRS => 10,
  CURLOPT_TIMEOUT => 0,
  CURLOPT_FOLLOWLOCATION => true,
  CURLOPT_HTTP_VERSION                =>
CURL_HTTP_VERSION_1_1,
  CURLOPT_CUSTOMREQUEST => 'POST',
  CURLOPT_POSTFIELDS =>'{"path":
    "/Slideshows/slideshow              x/'.
$zip_file_name.'"}',
  CURLOPT_HTTPHEADER => array(
    'Authorization: Bearer '.$access_token,
    'Content-Type: application/json',
    'Dropbox-API-Select-User: '.$team_user_id,
    'Dropbox-API-Path-Root:            {".tag":
"namespace_id", "namespace_id":
      "'.$namespace_id.'"}'
  ),
));
$response = curl_exec($curl);
curl_close($curl);
$response = json_decode($response, true);

sleep(1);[31]

$curl = curl_init();[32]
curl_setopt_array($curl, array(
  CURLOPT_URL =>
    'https://api.dropboxapi.com/2/files/
permanently_delete',
  CURLOPT_RETURNTRANSFER => true,
```

```
            CURLOPT_ENCODING => '',
            CURLOPT_MAXREDIRS => 10,
            CURLOPT_TIMEOUT => 0,
            CURLOPT_FOLLOWLOCATION => true,
            CURLOPT_HTTP_VERSION                    =>
CURL_HTTP_VERSION_1_1,
            CURLOPT_CUSTOMREQUEST => 'POST',
            CURLOPT_POSTFIELDS =>'{"path":
              "/Slideshows/slideshow x/'.$folder_name.'"}',
            CURLOPT_HTTPHEADER => array(
              'Authorization: Bearer '.$access_token,
              'Content-Type: application/json',
              'Dropbox-API-Select-User: '.$team_user_id,
              'Dropbox-API-Path-Root:              {".tag":
"namespace_id", "namespace_id":
                  '".$namespace_id.'"}'
            ),
          ));
          $response = curl_exec($curl);
          curl_close($curl);
      }

      echo "<br><div style='padding-left:50px; padding-
right:50px;'><center>
          Processed pending '".$folder_name.'" in 'slideshow
x' folder on Dropbox.
            </center></div><br>";
    }

    echo    "<br><br><br><center><h2>Finished    creating
slideshows.
        </h2></center><br>";
    echo   "<br><br><br><center><img   src='fireworks2.gif'
style='width:20px;'>
        </center></img>";
    exit;
```

```php
        } else {(18)
            echo '<br>';
            echo '<div>';
                echo '<center>';
                    echo '<form action="" method="post">';
                        echo '<input type="hidden" name="do" value="process">';
                        echo '<input type="submit" value="Process pending files"
                            class="button">';
                    echo '</form>';
                echo '</center>';
            echo '</div>';
        }
    }

    include('footer.php');(35)
?>
```

Code Explanation

1) ```php
<?php
include('header.php');
```

First of all PHP tags started and 'header.php' file is included.

2) ```php
if(isset($_COOKIE['user'])) {
    echo '<br> Welcome '.$_COOKIE['user'];
} else {
    $baseURL      =      'https://your-domain.com/projects/dropbox-to-dropbox/login.php';
    header("Location: $baseURL");
}
```

In this next part of code, it is checked if cookie related to login is set. It is used to verify if user is logged in. If user is logged in, then it will show message 'Welcome user'. Here 'user' is the email address of logged in user.

In case cookie is not set, it means that user is not logged in, then 'else' condition runs and immediately redirects the user to page 'login.php' using 'header()' function.

3) ```php
$client_id = "demo_client_id";
$client_secret = "demo_client_secret";
$namespace_id = "demo_namespace_id";
$team_user_id = "demo_team_user_id";
```

In next part of code, various variables are set. Here value of '$client_id' and '$client_secret' was received when app on Dropbox was created. Variables '$namespace_id' and '$team_user_id' has been created through other APIs which are no longer needed, so not included. This variable values will be used to run various APIs linked to Dropbox.

4) ```php
                          if(isset($_GET['access_token'])   &&   !empty($_GET['access_token'])){
```

$access_token = $_GET['access_token'];

Next part of code has been used to check the URL, if 'access_token' has been received, as sent by last file 'process-and-upload.php'. Code tries to get value of access_token using '$_GET' method and verifies that if it is set using 'isset()' function and verifies that if it's value received is not empty using '!empty()' function. If the variable is set and its value is not empty, then, it gets the value stored in variable 'access_token', using '$_GET' method and stores it inside variable '$access_token'. It will be used later in running APIs. In case, if value of access token is not received then step 17) runs.

```
5)    $curl = curl_init();
        curl_setopt_array($curl, array(
          CURLOPT_URL    =>    'https://api.dropboxapi.com/2/
files/list_folder',
          CURLOPT_RETURNTRANSFER => true,
          CURLOPT_ENCODING => '',
          CURLOPT_MAXREDIRS => 10,
          CURLOPT_TIMEOUT => 0,
          CURLOPT_FOLLOWLOCATION => true,
          CURLOPT_HTTP_VERSION                        =>
CURL_HTTP_VERSION_1_1,
          CURLOPT_CUSTOMREQUEST => 'POST',
          CURLOPT_POSTFIELDS
            =>'{"include_deleted":false,"include_has_explicit_sha
red_members":
            false,"include_media_info":true,"include_mounted_f
olders":
            true,"include_non_downloadable_files":false,"path":
            "/Slideshows/slideshow x","recursive":false}',
          CURLOPT_HTTPHEADER => array(
            'Authorization: Bearer '.$access_token."',
            'Content-Type: application/json',
            'Dropbox-API-Select-User: '.$team_user_id,
```

```
       'Dropbox-API-Path-Root:  {".tag":  "namespace_id",
"namespace_id":
              "'.$namespace_id.'"}'
   ),
 ));
 $response = curl_exec($curl);
 curl_close($curl);
 $response= json_decode($response, true);
```

After that, this API runs. This API has been used to list all files and folders in 'slideshow x' folder on Dropbox. In case of demo file, '#2222text.zip', if it has been unzipped, automatically on Dropbox's 'slideshow x' folder, then API response '$response' generates.

We convert the API response in variable '$response' from JSON to array() format using 'json_decode()' function. This response in array format has been shown below,

```
[entries] => Array
(
    [0] => Array
        (
            [.tag] => folder
            [name] => #2222test
            [path_lower] => /slideshows/slideshow x/#2222test
            [path_display] => /Slideshows/slideshow x/#2222test
            [parent_shared_folder_id] => 4709137073
            [id] => id:demogPAmZGsAAAAAAACURw
            [sharing_info] => Array
                (
                    [read_only] =>
                    [parent_shared_folder_id] => 4709137073
                    [traverse_only] =>
                    [no_access] =>
                )

        )

    [1] => Array
        (
            [.tag] => file
            [name] => #2222test.zip
```

[path_lower] => /slideshows/slideshow x/#2222test.zip
[path_display] => /Slideshows/slideshow x/#2222test.zip
[parent_shared_folder_id] => 4709137073
[id] => id:demogPAmZGsAAAAAAACURg
[client_modified] => 2023-12-14T19:30:09Z
[server_modified] => 2023-12-14T19:30:10Z
[rev] => 0160c7d4fe1b6930000000118afbab1
[size] => 526488
[sharing_info] => Array
    (
        [read_only] =>
        [parent_shared_folder_id] => 4709137073
        [modified_by] => dbid:demosbb5TpbW3swf90-
      116aQf67etjqtB8g
)

[is_downloadable] => 1
[content_hash]   =>
96acbd07f91f9b436634fef8b1dd7340cf246
)

)

[cursor]   =>   AAF5kd—
S6quBcSJWtCAG65Mm94SIXig3VYzw3v-8Z5pyq57tDDKswgjmgm-
    w5rncMUMfEu3-
yUypEV2eK2OiQEJ6Rc0ZWr2xyr3SURoAKIS0updLa-
    SdLrTOKBKCIfqYKWZzbJUBzoKp18o3hjstw6oH_gayKpkoZ6kaRd240
n6633343GY5mpE
    WULRCINV5jluBFU0JTU7zaOFyK7N1YSGcq2Hl2DscsaGOG9WM-KJU-
    qPfLUAAnUAmeJRmXnrrMKUCT-
w9KDpMQ5Z5a5az4sdKpAl6jvvshEcZts0YRJ9Yw
[has_more] =>

In the above API response, we can see that files and folders data is present inside [entries]. So, we can access data inside [entries] using variable '$response['entries']'.

We can further see that there is data available for one file and one folder at position [0] and [1].

6)   *if(empty($response['entries'])) {*
       *echo "

 <h1>Finished creating*
     *slideshows.</h1>
";*

> *echo "

 <img src='fireworks2.gif'*
> *style='width:20px;'> </img>";*
>   *exit;*
> *}*

After that, here 'if()' condition is set, it verifies using 'empty()' function, if response generated by above API is step 5) is empty, it means that there are no folders and files in 'slideshow x' folder and we can display message 'Finished creating slideshows.' Along with it a small image named 'fireworks2.gif' has been displayed using 'img' tag of HTML.

In the end, 'exit' runs, which avoid running any further code of this file.

7)   *$names = array();*
>   *foreach($response['entries'] as $getnames){*
>   *if (strpos($getnames['name'], ".") !== false) { } else {*
>   *$names[] = $getnames['name'];*
>   *}*
>   *}*

In case, response of API, in step 5) was not empty, if means there are folders and files which need processed. This code uses 'foreach()' loop to get all folder and files names one by one from 'slideshow x' folder on Dropbox and put in variable '$getnames', to run further operations on each of these folders. In this case, '$getnames' tries to access inner value of '[name]' inside each '[0]' and '[1]', which will have value as follows,

$getnames['name'] = '#2222test' // on first run

$getnames['name'] = '#2222test.zip' // on second run

After that 'strpos()' function is used to verify if dot '.' is included in any of that folder or file name, then exclude it. It is done because there are zip files as well whose name contains '.zip' in it, and we do not want to include those zip files, either they are unzipped yet or not unzipped yet.

In case dot '.' is not present in folder names collected, then save them in another variable '$names'. In above case, the one with dot '.' will be saved in '$names' variable, as below,

$names = [0] => '#2222test'

If there are multiple folder names, then they all get saved, in variable '$names'.

8) *$unique_names = array_unique($names);*

In the next part of code 'array_unique()' function used, so that any duplicate values in variable '$names' are removed and saved in another variable '$unique_names'.

$unique_names = [0] => '#2222test'

9) *foreach($unique_names as $folder_name){*
   $zip_file_name = $folder_name.'.zip';
       $from_path = "/Slideshows/slideshow x/$folder_name/ files/slideshow x";
       $to_path = "/Slideshows/Slideshows created/ $folder_name";

In the next part of code, 'foreach()' loop has been used to go through each folder name, present in variable '$unique_names' and it will be stored in variable '$folder_name'.

After that, another variable '$zip_file_name' holds value of '$folder_name' variable and adds '.zip' in end of it. In this way, we will trigger only those zip files, which are unzipped, when this code runs.

In the next part of code, variables '$from_path' and '$to_path' are created, which includes value of variable '$folder_name', as follows,

$folder_name = '#2222test' //Demo variable value

$from_path = '/Slideshows/slideshow x/#2222test/files/ slideshow x'

$to_path = '/Slideshows/Slideshows created/#2222test'

```
10)     $curl = curl_init();
            curl_setopt_array($curl, array(
            CURLOPT_URL  =>  'https://api.dropboxapi.com/2/
files/move_v2',
            CURLOPT_RETURNTRANSFER => true,
            CURLOPT_ENCODING => '',
            CURLOPT_MAXREDIRS => 10,
            CURLOPT_TIMEOUT => 0,
            CURLOPT_FOLLOWLOCATION => true,
            CURLOPT_HTTP_VERSION                    =>
CURL_HTTP_VERSION_1_1,
            CURLOPT_CUSTOMREQUEST => 'POST',
            CURLOPT_POSTFIELDS
            =>'{"allow_ownership_transfer":true,"allow_share
d_folder":
            true,"autorename":true,"from_path":"'.
$from_path.'","to_path":
            "'.$to_path.'"}',
            CURLOPT_HTTPHEADER => array(
            'Authorization: Bearer '.$access_token.'',
            'Content-Type: application/json',
            'Dropbox-API-Select-User: '.$team_user_id,
            'Dropbox-API-Path-Root: {".tag": "namespace_id",
"namespace_id":
                '".$namespace_id.'"}'
            ),
            ));
            $response_move = curl_exec($curl);
            curl_close($curl);
            $response_move = json_decode($response_move, true);
```

In the next part of code, an API is run, which move all folders from 'slideshow x' folder using variable '$from_path' on

Dropbox to 'Slideshows created' folder using variable '$to_path' as created in step 9). After moving the all files of a folder, it generates a response. Response has been saved inside variable '$response_move'. After that 'json_decode()' function has been used, which is used to convert value of '$response_move' variable from JSON format to array format. Data in array format is shown below,

```
[metadata] => Array
    (
        [.tag] => folder
        [name] => #2222test
        [path_lower] => /slideshows/slideshows created/#2222test
        [path_display] => /Slideshows/Slideshows created/#2222test
        [parent_shared_folder_id] => 4709137073
        [id] => id:demogPAmZGsAAAAAACUSQ
        [sharing_info] => Array
            (
                [read_only] =>
                [parent_shared_folder_id] => 4709137073
                [traverse_only] =>
                [no_access] =>
            )

    )
```

In this response generated, we can see that data is inside [metadata] and if we want to read name of folder whose data has been moved, then it is inside [name]. To read folder name, we can read it using variable '$response_move['metadata']['name']'.

11) *if(isset($response_move['metadata']['name']) &&*
    !empty($response_move['metadata']['name'])){

In next part of code, it is verified that the response generated from API in step 10), is set using 'isset()' function and not empty using '!empty()' function. If variable is verified and found present, then next part of code runs at step 12), else step 16) runs.

```
12)        $curl = curl_init();
                curl_setopt_array($curl, array(
                  CURLOPT_URL =>
                  'https://api.dropboxapi.com/2/files/
permanently_delete',
                  CURLOPT_RETURNTRANSFER => true,
                  CURLOPT_ENCODING => '',
                  CURLOPT_MAXREDIRS => 10,
                  CURLOPT_TIMEOUT => 0,
                  CURLOPT_FOLLOWLOCATION => true,
                  CURLOPT_HTTP_VERSION                    =>
CURL_HTTP_VERSION_1_1,
                  CURLOPT_CUSTOMREQUEST => 'POST',
                  CURLOPT_POSTFIELDS =>'{"path":
                  "/Slideshows/slideshow x/'.$zip_file_name.'"}',
                  CURLOPT_HTTPHEADER => array(
                  'Authorization: Bearer '.$access_token,
                  'Content-Type: application/json',
                  'Dropbox-API-Select-User: '.$team_user_id,
                  'Dropbox-API-Path-Root:               {".tag":
"namespace_id", "namespace_id":
                      "'.$namespace_id.'"}'
                  ),
                ));
                $response = curl_exec($curl);
                curl_close($curl);
                $response = json_decode($response, true);
```

In next part of code, this API runs, which deletes the zip file, which was saved in variable '$zip_file_name' as set in step 9).

13) *sleep(1);*

It has been observed during testing that step 14) was unable to run sometimes because of possible reason that above API is still in the middle of processing, so 'sleep()' function has been set here, which waits for 1 second before processing next step.

```
14)      $curl = curl_init();
            curl_setopt_array($curl, array(
              CURLOPT_URL =>
              'https://api.dropboxapi.com/2/files/
permanently_delete',
              CURLOPT_RETURNTRANSFER => true,
              CURLOPT_ENCODING => '',
              CURLOPT_MAXREDIRS => 10,
              CURLOPT_TIMEOUT => 0,
              CURLOPT_FOLLOWLOCATION => true,
              CURLOPT_HTTP_VERSION              =>
CURL_HTTP_VERSION_1_1,
              CURLOPT_CUSTOMREQUEST => 'POST',
              CURLOPT_POSTFIELDS =>'{"path":
                "/Slideshows/slideshow x/'.$folder_name.'"}',
              CURLOPT_HTTPHEADER => array(
                'Authorization: Bearer '.$access_token,
                'Content-Type: application/json',
                'Dropbox-API-Select-User: '.$team_user_id,
                'Dropbox-API-Path-Root:              {".tag":
"namespace_id", "namespace_id":
                  "'.$namespace_id.'"}'
              ),
            ));
            $response = curl_exec($curl);
            curl_close($curl);
      }
```

In next part of code, API runs, which delete the folder name from 'slideshow x' folder on Dropbox. This folder name has been saved in variable '$folder_name' as created in step 9).

15) echo "
<div style='padding-left:50px; padding-right:50px;'><center>Processed
        pending "'.$folder_name.'" in 'slideshow x' folder on

Dropbox.</center></div>

";

In next part of code, it is shown message that "Processed pending '$folder_name' in 'slideshow x' folder on Dropbox'. Here '$folder_name' variable value is received from step 9). This message displays for each folder which has been processed by this code, which includes moving files and deleting zip file and folder name on Dropbox. Message for each folder processed in shown in a separate line, as follows,

Processed pending '#2222test' in 'slideshow x' folder on Dropbox.

16)   *echo "

<center><h1>Finished creating slideshows.</h1></center>
";*
        *echo   "

<center><img src='fireworks2.gif'*
        style='width:20px;'></center></img>";
        exit;

In the next part of code, it displays message 'Finished creating slideshows.' And at bottom of this text, it displays an image named 'fireworks2.gif'. Message shows as follows,

Finished creating slideshows.

Below it is 'exit' used, which stops running any further code of this file after it.

17) *} else {*
    *echo "

<center>Moves files from 'slideshow x' folder to*
    'Slideshows created' folder. </center>";
    *echo "

<div style='padding-left:50px; padding-right:50px;'><center>It*

is observed that sometimes because of heavy files Dropbox's automated

'unzip' function takes longer in 'slideshow x' folder on Dropbox and some

operations not performed because of this reason. In this case, files are still

present in 'slideshow x' folder and for further processing, this page can be

used to complete pending tasks, in series, for all unzipped slideshows at

ones, by below button.</center></div>";

In next part of code 'else' runs, which is linked to step 4). In case 'access_token' is missing in URL, in that case, follow part of code runs. This part of code runs, when menu button 'Move files Uploaded' is pressed. On top of page, it displays a message explaining why this page is useful. Message displayed is "It is observed that sometimes because of heavy files Dropbox's automated 'unzip' function takes longer in 'slideshow x' folder on Dropbox and some operations not performed because of this reason. In this case, files are still present in 'slideshow x' folder and for further processing, this page can be used to complete pending tasks, in series, for all unzipped slideshows at ones, by below button.". It's output shows as follows,

Moves files from 'slideshow x' folder to 'Slideshows created' folder.

It is observed that sometimes because of heavy files Dropbox's automated 'unzip' function takes longer in 'slideshow x' folder on Dropbox and some operations not performed because of this reason. In this case, files are still present in 'slideshow x' folder and for further processing, this page

can be used to complete pending tasks, in series, for all unzipped slideshows at ones, by below button.

Button discussed in above paragraph, it is present at the end of file 'move_files_uploaded.php' and not after this code. It is because the next part of code runs, when button is pressed. So, below that code has been explained first which shows button.

```
18) } else {
        echo '<br>';
        echo '<div>';
            echo '<center>';
                echo '<form action="" method="post">';
                    echo '<input type="hidden" name="do" value="process">';

                    echo '<input type="submit" value="Process pending files"

                        class="button">';
                echo '</form>';
            echo '</center>';
        echo '</div>';
    }
```

In above code, we can see that it is working on condition 'else' and 'if' condition will be explained in step 19).

After else condition '<br>' tag has been added. It is used to display output of next part of code in next line.

After that a '<div>' tag has been created and placed in '<center>' tag which will cause the output of code to display only at the middle of the page.

After that a form has been created whose action is set to "", which is empty, so this page will send the output data to current page and 'method' used is 'POST', so in case we want to get the output of form after button is pressed, we need to use '$_POST' method to get output of this form.

After that input '<input>' field has been created of type 'hidden', so it will not be visible on output page. Its name is set to 'do' and value is set to 'process'. When button is pressed, then we can read the 'name' and 'value' of this field.

In the next line, '<input type="submit">' has been created. It is the button created, and value given is 'Process pending files', so this value will show on the button, as text. We have also given a class as 'button' to this button, which will be used to change design of this button, as per coding defined for class '.button' in 'header.php' file. When this button is pressed, this 'form' output can be fetched in step 19).

Below this code various tags are closed. First 'form' tag is closed '</form>', then 'center' tag is closed '</center>' and then 'div' tag is closed '</div>'.

19) **if(isset($_POST['do']) && !empty($_POST['do'])){**

In next part of code, when button gets pressed, as mentioned in step 18), we try to fetch value of variable name 'do' using '$_POST' method. Further it is verified that value of 'do' is set using 'isset()' function and is not empty, using '!empty()' function.

20) *$refresh_token = "demo_refresh_token 3CuDBxzj6lhwFdQV8uoE-OL";*

After that a variable '$refresh_token' has been assigned with 'Refresh Token'.

21)   *$curl = curl_init();*
           curl_setopt_array($curl, array(
            CURLOPT_URL   =>   'https://api.dropbox.com/ oauth2/token',
            CURLOPT_RETURNTRANSFER => true,
            CURLOPT_ENCODING => '',
            CURLOPT_MAXREDIRS => 10,
            CURLOPT_TIMEOUT => 0,
            CURLOPT_FOLLOWLOCATION => true,

```
CURLOPT_HTTP_VERSION                    =>
CURL_HTTP_VERSION_1_1,
        CURLOPT_CUSTOMREQUEST => 'POST',
        CURLOPT_POSTFIELDS                =>
'grant_type=refresh_token&refresh_token=
        '.$refresh_token.'&client_id='.
$client_id.'&client_secret='.$client_secret.",
        CURLOPT_HTTPHEADER => array(
        'Content-Type:            application/x-www-form-
urlencoded'
        ),
        ));
        $response = curl_exec($curl);
        curl_close($curl);
        $response = json_decode($response, true);
```

In above API, we use the variable '$refresh_token' along with '$client_id' and '$client_secret' and try to get the response generated by API in '$response' variable. This code has been used to generate access token. After that 'json_decode()' function is used to convert API response from JSON to array format. It converts the response in the form of array, as shown below,

```
[access_token] => demo_access_token
    wVd4zWAe4Uaq4sgfAGWkjo9SYnHlg1Y0crzP_AsqSIOCfn8Uyf7a6N
XrLERWfdxAqUBb
    tDCQmVPM5iKGmpRdz9IszmOSLfFJXfWJim0Q0jH_xM4wUz9pBvSO
nf8rNdeyTDSC6Xst-
    9mccVX2N-S
    [token_type] => bearer
    [expires_in] => 14400
```

In above API response, it is visible that 'access_token' is present inside [access_token]. We can get value of access token using '$response['access_token']. As shown in above response, this 'access_token' has a life span of 14400 seconds.

14400/60 = 240 minutes

240/60 = 4 hours // This access_token is not reusable after 4 hours of generating

22) *if(!empty($response['access_token'])){*
          $access_token = $response['access_token'];
        } else {
          echo "Dropbox Access Token missing. It could be because of temporary
                network error, refresh token may've expired, etc. Please retry after
                some   time   or   contact   this   software administrator.";
          exit;
        }

In this code, first it is verified using 'if()' condition that output of variable '$response['access_token']' is not empty, using '!empty()' function. After that, if it is found not empty, then value of '$response['access_token']' variable is stored inside another variable '$access_token'.

In case the value of '$response' is found empty, then it will show message 'Dropbox Access Token missing. It could be because of temporary network error, refresh token may've expired, etc. Please retry after some time or contact this software administrator.'

Dropbox Access Token missing. It could be because of temporary network error, refresh token may've expired, etc. Please retry after some time or contact this software administrator.

In case the access token failed to generate, then there are three solutions listed for it, under topic 'Dropbox App Details'.

In case 'access_token' generated through Dropbox App, then it has a soft life span of only 4 hours until it is valid to use, as mentioned in step 21).

In case of solution offered to generate 'access_token' through 'refresh_token' and other details, it is already implemented in this software and working good, so far.

In case 'refresh_token' need regenerated, through oauth2 setup by manual login to Dropbox and verifying, as mentioned under topic 'Oauth2 Setup' then it automatically saves new 'refresh_token' in database, however it needs to be manually added in code and if we do not want to add in manually, then under topic 'Index.php', some code has been commented in step 6). It can be uncommented to get 'refresh_token' from database automatically. This code is commented, just to keep the work load lower, on this software, because it will make a database call every time to fetch refresh token from there and it can be avoided, at the moment.

Other possible solutions are already listed in message which is to retry after some time may fix this issue automatically or can contact software administrator, to look into the possible cause of issue and fix it in best possible way.

After that 'exit' has been used, so that in case '$response' is empty and 'Access Token' is not generated, then next part of code will not run.

```
23)     $curl = curl_init();
            curl_setopt_array($curl, array(
            CURLOPT_URL  =>  'https://api.dropboxapi.com/2/
files/list_folder',
            CURLOPT_RETURNTRANSFER => true,
            CURLOPT_ENCODING => '',
            CURLOPT_MAXREDIRS => 10,
            CURLOPT_TIMEOUT => 0,
            CURLOPT_FOLLOWLOCATION => true,
            CURLOPT_HTTP_VERSION                            =>
CURL_HTTP_VERSION_1_1,
            CURLOPT_CUSTOMREQUEST => 'POST',
            CURLOPT_POSTFIELDS
              =>'{"include_deleted":false,"include_has_explicit_s
```

```
hared_members":
                false,"include_media_info":true,"include_mounted
_folders":
                true,"include_non_downloadable_files":false,"path
":
                "/Slideshows/slideshow x","recursive":false}',
            CURLOPT_HTTPHEADER => array(
                'Authorization: Bearer '.$access_token.'",
                'Content-Type: application/json',
                'Dropbox-API-Select-User: '.$team_user_id,
                'Dropbox-API-Path-Root:               {".tag":
"namespace_id", "namespace_id":
                    "'.$namespace_id.'"}'
            ),
        ));
        $response = curl_exec($curl);
        curl_close($curl);
        $response= json_decode($response, true);
```

In the next part of code, an API has been run, which is used to list all files and folders present in 'slideshow x' folder on Dropbox.

Later, the response generated in variable '$response', has been converted from JSON to array type using 'json_decode()' function. Response generated from this API, has been shown below,

```
[entries] => Array
  (
     [0] => Array
        (
            [.tag] => folder
            [name] => #2222test
            [path_lower] => /slideshows/slideshow x/#2222test
            [path_display] => /Slideshows/slideshow x/#2222test
            [parent_shared_folder_id] => 4709137073
            [id] => id:demogPAmZGsAAAAAAACURw
            [sharing_info] => Array
```

```
                (
                    [read_only] =>
                    [parent_shared_folder_id] => 4709137073
                    [traverse_only] =>
                    [no_access] =>
                )

        )

    [1] => Array
        (
            [.tag] => file
            [name] => #2222test.zip
            [path_lower] => /slideshows/slideshow x/#2222test.zip
            [path_display] => /Slideshows/slideshow x/#2222test.zip
            [parent_shared_folder_id] => 4709137073
            [id] => demogPAmZGsAAAAAAACURg
            [client_modified] => 2023-12-14T19:30:09Z
            [server_modified] => 2023-12-14T19:30:10Z
            [rev] => 0160c7d4fe1b6930000000118afbab1
            [size] => 526488
            [sharing_info] => Array
                (
                    [read_only] =>
                    [parent_shared_folder_id] => 4709137073
                    [modified_by] => dbid:demosbb5TpbW3swf90-
                    116aQf67etjqtB8g
                )

            [is_downloadable] => 1
            [content_hash]                                        =>
96acbd07f91f9b436634fef8b1dd7340cf246
        )

    )

    [cursor]                              =>                     AAF5kd—
S6quBcSJWtCAG65Mm94SIXig3VYzw3v-8Z5pyq57tDDKswgjmgm-
    w5rncMUMfEu3-
yUypEV2eK2OiQEJ6Rc0ZWr2xyr3SUR0AKIS0updLa-
    SdLrTOKBKCIfqYKWZzbJUBzoKp18o3hjstw6oH_gayKpkoZ6kaRd240
n663334a3Y5mpE
    WULRCINV5jluBFU0JTU7zaOFyK7N1YSGcq2Hl2DscsaGOG9WM-KJU-
    qPfLUAAnUAmeJRmXnrrMKUCT-
w9KDpMQ5Z5a5az4sdKpAl6jvvshEcZts0YRJ9Yw
    [has_more] =>
```

This response is based on single zip file '#2222test.zip' and its related folder '#2222test'. We can see in above response that it is present inside [entries] array. So, inner data of response can be accessed using, '$response['entries']'.

24)   *if(empty($response['entries'])) {*
            *echo '
<center>No pending files to process.</center>';*
            exit;
        }

After that this code runs which verifies, if value of variable '$response['entries']' is empty, using 'empty()' function. In case it is empty, it will show following message,

No pending files to process.

After that 'exit' has been used which stops the processing of further code.

25)   *$names = array();*
            foreach($response['entries'] as $getnames){
                if (strpos($getnames['name'], ".") !== false) { } else {
                    $names[] = $getnames['name'];
                }
            }

This code runs, if API at step 23) do not have an empty response. In this code, first variable named '$names' has been initialized as empty array(). After that 'foreach()' loop has been used which go through entries in array variable '$response' at path ['entries'] and temporarily stores values of each output in another variable '$getnames'. We can see in above example at step 23), that '[name] =>' contains name of zip file and folder name. We can access those names using '$getnames['name']'.

After that, 'strpos()' function has been used to check in each file and folder name, stored in variable "$getnames['name']" that if it contains a dot '.' in its name. It is checked because zip files present in folder 'slideshow x' has extension '.zip' and it contains a dot '.', while folder names do not contain any extension with dot '.'. So, in case it do not contain dot '.', then 'else' condition runs. We save all the folder names from variable '$getnames' at path ['name'] to '$names' variable. Here '[]' has been added at end of '$names[]' variable because it is of type array and to get values in array type variable, we use '[]'. In case of output generated by API, at step 23), following will be stored in '$names' variable,

$names = [0] => '#2222test'

26) *$unique_names = array_unique($names);*

After that, this code runs, in which function 'array_unique()' has been used on '$names' variable. It ensures that '$names' variable do not have any duplicate names, in case there are duplicate names, they get removed by function 'array_unique()' function and it's value has been saved in another variable '$unique_names'. Output will be as follow,

$unique_names = [0] => '#2222test'

27)   *foreach($unique_names as $folder_name){*
             $zip_file_name = $folder_name.'.zip';
             $from_path   =   "/Slideshows/slideshow   x/ $folder_name/files/slideshow x";
             $to_path   =   "/Slideshows/Slideshows   created/ $folder_name";

In the next part of code, we are using 'foreach()' loop, which will go through all the folder names present in variable '$unique_names' and temporarily store them, one by one, in variable '$folder_name' for further processing.

After that, from that folder name, which has been unzipped in 'slideshow x' folder on Dropbox, we add '.zip', in end of it and save it in another variable '$zip_file_name'. This method has been used to completely ignore those zip files, which are not unzipped yet. So, it will cause processing of code in next steps, only on unzipped files.

In next part of code '$from_path' and '$to_path' has been created. Values of these variables, will be on basis of data generated in step 26), as shown below,

$zip_file_name = '#2222test.zip'

$from_path = '/Slideshows/slideshow x/#2222test/files/ slideshow x'

$to_path = '/Slideshows/Slideshows created/#2222test'

```
28)     $curl = curl_init();
            curl_setopt_array($curl, array(
            CURLOPT_URL              =>              'https://
api.dropboxapi.com/2/files/move_v2',
            CURLOPT_RETURNTRANSFER => true,
            CURLOPT_ENCODING => '',
            CURLOPT_MAXREDIRS => 10,
            CURLOPT_TIMEOUT => 0,
            CURLOPT_FOLLOWLOCATION => true,
            CURLOPT_HTTP_VERSION              =>
CURL_HTTP_VERSION_1_1,
            CURLOPT_CUSTOMREQUEST => 'POST',
            CURLOPT_POSTFIELDS
             =>'{"allow_ownership_transfer":true,"allow_sha
red_folder":
            true,"autorename":true,"from_path":"'.
$from_path.'","to_path":
            "'.$to_path.'"}',
            CURLOPT_HTTPHEADER => array(
            'Authorization: Bearer '.$access_token.'',
            'Content-Type: application/json',
            'Dropbox-API-Select-User: '.$team_user_id,
            'Dropbox-API-Path-Root:              {".tag":
```

```
"namespace_id", "namespace_id":
            "'.$namespace_id.'"}'
        ),
    ));
    $response_move = curl_exec($curl);
    curl_close($curl);
    $response_move = json_decode($response_move,
true);
```

In next step, API has been run, which will move files from path mentioned in '$from_path' variable, to path mentioned in '$to_path' variable, in step 27).

Response generated by above API, has been saved in variable '$response_move'. After that 'json_decode()' function has been used to convert response from JSON format to array() format. Following is the response generated in array format,

```
[metadata] => Array
    (
        [.tag] => folder
        [name] => #2222test
        [path_lower] => /slideshows/slideshows created/#2222test
        [path_display] => /Slideshows/Slideshows created/#2222test
        [parent_shared_folder_id] => 4709137073
        [id] => id:demogPAmZGsAAAAAAACUSQ
        [sharing_info] => Array
            (
                [read_only] =>
                [parent_shared_folder_id] => 4709137073
                [traverse_only] =>
                [no_access] =>
            )

    )
```

In above response generated, we can see that folder name is saved in [name], is present in another array [metadata] whose data has been successfully moved to 'Slideshows created' folder on Dropbox. We can access this folder name using '$response_move['metadata']['name']'.

29) *if(isset($response_move['metadata']['name']) &&*
  !empty($response_move['metadata']['name'])){

In next part of code, it has been verified that if data in variable '$response_move['metadata']['name'] is set, using 'isset()' function and value of this variable is not empty, using '! empty()' function, then next step of code will run.

30)   *$curl = curl_init();*
      curl_setopt_array($curl, array(
      CURLOPT_URL =>
      'https://api.dropboxapi.com/2/files/
permanently_delete',
      CURLOPT_RETURNTRANSFER => true,
      CURLOPT_ENCODING => '',
      CURLOPT_MAXREDIRS => 10,
      CURLOPT_TIMEOUT => 0,
      CURLOPT_FOLLOWLOCATION => true,
      CURLOPT_HTTP_VERSION   =>
CURL_HTTP_VERSION_1_1,
      CURLOPT_CUSTOMREQUEST => 'POST',
      CURLOPT_POSTFIELDS =>'{"path":
      "/Slideshows/slideshow   x/'.
$zip_file_name.'"}',
      CURLOPT_HTTPHEADER => array(
      'Authorization: Bearer '.$access_token,
      'Content-Type: application/json',
      'Dropbox-API-Select-User: '.$team_user_id,
      'Dropbox-API-Path-Root: {".tag":
"namespace_id", "namespace_id":
      "'.$namespace_id.'"}'
      ),
      ));
      $response = curl_exec($curl);

```
curl_close($curl);
$response = json_decode($response, true);
```

In this step, an API runs, which will delete zip file, saved in variable '$zip_file_name', in step 27) from folder 'slideshow x' on Dropbox.

31) *sleep(1);*

After that 'sleep()' function has been used to delay the processing of next part of code, by one second. It has been used because during testing, it has been observed that next API in step 32) didn't work rarely because of possible reason of last API was in processing stage in step 30). So, a delay of 1 second has been set, before processing API in step 32).

32)
```
$curl = curl_init();
curl_setopt_array($curl, array(
    CURLOPT_URL =>
        'https://api.dropboxapi.com/2/files/
permanently_delete',
    CURLOPT_RETURNTRANSFER => true,
    CURLOPT_ENCODING => '',
    CURLOPT_MAXREDIRS => 10,
    CURLOPT_TIMEOUT => 0,
    CURLOPT_FOLLOWLOCATION => true,
    CURLOPT_HTTP_VERSION           =>
CURL_HTTP_VERSION_1_1,
    CURLOPT_CUSTOMREQUEST => 'POST',
    CURLOPT_POSTFIELDS =>'{"path":
        "/Slideshows/slideshow x/".$folder_name."'}',
    CURLOPT_HTTPHEADER => array(
        'Authorization: Bearer '.$access_token,
        'Content-Type: application/json',
        'Dropbox-API-Select-User: '.$team_user_id,
        'Dropbox-API-Path-Root:           {".tag":
```

```
"namespace_id", "namespace_id":
                "'".$namespace_id."'"}'
        ),
        ));
        $response = curl_exec($curl);
        curl_close($curl);
    }
```

In next step, API has been run, which deletes folder name as per saved in variable '$folder_name' in step 27), from 'slideshow x' folder on Dropbox.

33)   *echo "
 *
Processed pending '".$folder_name."'" in 'slideshow x' folder on Dropbox.
*
";*
    }

In next part of code, a message has been displayed, "Processed pending '$folder_name' in 'slideshow x' folder on Dropbox." It has been shown as follows,

Processed pending '#2222test' in 'slideshow
x' folder on Dropbox.

Step 27) to 33) repeats and message similar to one shown above repeats for each folder name, until all the pending folders on 'slideshow x' folder has been processed on the Dropbox.

34)   *echo "

 <h2>Finished creating slideshows.*
    *</h2>
";*
    *echo "

 <img src='fireworks2.gif' style='width:20px;'>*
    * </img>";*
    exit;

In this next code, it displays the message 'Finished creating slideshows.' and below it a .gif image has been added using '<img>' tag, whose width is set to 20 pixels using inline css.

Finished creating slideshows.

In the end, 'exit' has been used, stop any processing of any further code.

35) *include('footer.php');*
    ?>

In next part of code, it includes 'footer.php' file and closes PHP tag using '?>'.

ADDITIONAL FILES USED

There are other files present in project which are not listed and not explained in details, in topic,

1) .htaccess: It has been used to do setting on server to run latest version of PHP.

2) jquery-3.7.1.min.js: This file contains the javascript library which make us capable to add and run Jquery related code in project.

3) fireworks2.gif: Image file included.

REFERENCES

1) Dropbox HTTP API reference guide: https://www.dropbox.com/developers/documentation/http/documentation

2) Dropbox Team Files guide: https://developers.dropbox.com/dbx-team-files-guide

3) Dropbox File Access guide: https://developers.dropbox.com/dbx-file-access-guide

4) Dropbox API support: https://www.dropboxforum.com/t5/Dropbox-API-Support-Feedback/bd-p/101000014

5) Dropbox app setup: https://www.dropbox.com/developers/apps

6) PHP reference guide: https://www.php.net/manual/en/intro-whatis.php

7) HTML reference guide: https://www.youtube.com/watch?v=iCoiTjJJeUI&list=PLGnR7Ae9qkw77Mztjx6NvNq5GZZBMY0pw

8) CSS reference guide: https://developer.mozilla.org/en-US/docs/Web/CSS

9) Jquery reference guide: https://learn.jquery.com/

10) Regex reference guide: https://coderpad.io/blog/development/the-complete-guide-to-regular-expressions-regex/

THANK YOU